Bought in Budapest, Hungary Sept 20, 2013
Bible Book store

Anti-Semitism

ANTI-SEMITISM

R. B. THIEME, JR.

R. B. THIEME, JR., BIBLE MINISTRIES
HOUSTON, TEXAS

This book is edited from the lectures and unpublished notes of R. B. Thieme, Jr.

A catalog of available tapes and publications will be provided upon request

R. B. Thieme, Jr., Bible Ministries
5139 West Alabama, Houston, Texas 77056

Printed in the United States of America

ISBN 1-55764-048-3

Dedication

To Jewish friends, old and new, this volume is respectfully and affectionately dedicated.

Barry Goldwater, gentleman, officer, statesman, with whom it was a pleasure to serve in those wartime years.

Dr. Charles L. Feinberg, Hebrew scholar and professor, who made the original languages of the Old Testament so live in the classroom that exegesis became my way of life.

Contents

Chapter 1
The Middle East Crucible

Chapter 2
The Source of Anti-Semitism

Chapter 3
Anti-Semitism in Ancient History

Chapter 4
Anti-Semitism in Modern History

Chapter 5
The Biblical View of Anti-Semitism

Chapter 6
The Unique Jew

Chapter 7
Applying Biblical Principles to Anti-Semitism

Prologue

IN HIS SCHOLARLY BOOK *Semites & Anti-Semites*, Bernard Lewis presents three categories of hostility directed toward Jews. The first is opposition to Israel as a nation, to her foreign policy, or to Zionism, as a political and religious ideology, without necessarily being inspired by prejudice. The second category is "normal" prejudice, which is often directed against those of another tribe, another race, another faith, or from another place. This second category includes the attitudes which majorities sometimes adopt toward minorities. The third category of enmity portrays the Jew as the root of virtually all evil in the world, engaged in an eternal and universal conspiracy, to infiltrate, corrupt, and ultimately rule the gentile world. This third category includes the desire of the anti-Semite to castigate, eliminate, and finally to physically exterminate the Jew.[1]

---

1. Bernard Lewis, *Semites & Anti-Semites* (New York: W. W. Norton & Co., 1986), pp. 20–23.

Anti-Semitism was originally published by R. B. Thieme, Jr., in 1974 as a warning against the misguided, detestable, and anti-Christian nature of the latter two categories of antagonism toward Jews. People may legitimately differ with the foreign policy of Israel or reject an individual Jew, as long as that disagreement or rejection is not motivated by anti-Semitism. However, since the completion of this book seventeen years ago, animosity against Jews has advanced well beyond disagreement with the national aspirations of Israel or rejection of individual Jews. The noxious forms of anti-Semitism have increased dramatically.

In 1975 the United Nations General Assembly passed a resolution defining Zionism as a "form of racism and racial discrimination." Racism, the universal epithet that conveys an inherent superiority of one race over another, was ironically turned against the Jew. According to A. M. Rosenthal, the racism label has since been used against the Jews by Israel-hating governments and anti-Semitic officials around the world to spread fear and irrational hatred among their own people.[2]

Since established as a national entity in 1948, Israel has been forced into war, compelled to fight or be driven into the sea. Throughout the 1980's, however, many Western governments have demanded that Israel conform to standards of behavior appropriate to a nation at peace. Undoubtedly, these same nations if faced with similar threats of annihilation would react not unlike Israel. In fact, Charles Krauthammer notes that in less serious conflicts certain countries have shown even less restraint toward their enemies than Israel now displays toward the Palestinians.[3] He cites as examples the British during the Arab Revolt of 1936–39, the French in Algeria in the 1950's, and India's repression of the Sikhs in 1984.

These remarks describing Israel's restraint are not cited to excuse actual misdeeds, but to expose a double standard. Israel must comply with a norm of conduct that other governments would not require of themselves. The hypocrisy of castigating Israel for behavior that is acceptable to these nations in corresponding

---

2. *New York Times*, 19 December 1989.

3. "Judging Israel," *Time*, 26 February 1990, pp. 77–78.

circumstances betrays a discriminatory standard. The word for that discrimination is anti-Semitism.[4]

The world press spends a disproportionate amount of time scrutinizing Israel. Minor skirmishes between Israel and her Arab neighbors are extensively reported, while the war between Iraq and Iran, one of the bloodiest in this century with over a million casualties, passed with far less attention.[5] During the 1989–90 Palestinian uprising, news services were quick to report any Palestinian killed by Israelis. But the fact that more Palestinians have died at the hands of their brother Palestinians than by the Israelis was buried on a back page or ignored entirely.[6]

Bernard Lewis observes that the Arab war against Israel has become generalized as a war against all Jews. As proof he quotes excerpts from certain literature, textbooks, and newspapers of Islamic and Arab nations which depict Jews collectively as hostile, malevolent, subhuman.[7] This is the traditional stereotypical language of anti-Semitism. In addition, censorship by Arab governments or by Arab journalists often eliminates any portrayal of Jews in a favorable light.

Anti-Semitic incidents, such as the promotion of Jewish conspiracy propaganda in Sweden by "Radio Islam," actual threats against Jews in Leningrad and Moscow, and attacks on synagogues in Romania and France, are becoming commonplace. In Soviet Russia the rise of nationalism parallels the rise of atavistic prejudice and is creating fear among Russian Jews of a new pogrom. Even Poland and Hungary, which had their Jewish populations exterminated in the Nazi Holocaust, are exhibiting signs of rekindled anti-Semitism.

The United States has not remained unaffected by the rise of anti-Semitism. Pseudo-Christian groups called "Identity Churches," which encompass the Christian Defense League, Aryan Nations,

---

4. Krauthammer, "Judging Israel," p. 78.

5. Lewis, *Semites & Anti-Semites*, p. 13.

6. Krauthammer, "Judging Israel," p. 78.

7. Lewis, *Semites & Anti-Semites*, pp. 214–35.

Christian Patriots Defense League, and certain elements of the Ku Klux Klan, are perpetuating the myth that Jews are responsible for world problems. Louis Farrakhan, leader of the Black Muslim group "Nation of Islam," calls Judaism "a gutter religion" and declares Hitler "a great man."[8] The neo-Nazi "Skinhead" movement grows ever more visible and vocal. At the same time, the Anti-Defamation League of B'nai B'rith reports that anti-Semitic incidents in 1989, ranging from desecration to murder, have reached their highest level in eleven years.[9]

Neither the United States nor any other nation can afford anti-Semitism. The Scriptures state that God curses those who curse Israel (Gen. 12:3), and that promise to Israel from God remains immutable to this very day. God reserves the sovereign right to punish the Jews for disobedience (Lev. 26:14–39; Deut. 28:15–68), but throughout their history He has preserved this race of people because of His promise (Gen. 12:1–3; cf., Lev. 26:44). Israel has a guaranteed national future which no human or satanic machinations can destroy.

The Jewish race was founded on the principle of belief in the promise of God (Gen. 15:6; cf., Rom. 4:1–5). Abraham, the father of the Jewish race, "believed in the Lord; and He [God] reckoned it to him as righteousness." The promise begins with salvation by the grace of God through faith in Jesus Christ (Eph. 2:8–9). This is the legacy of Abraham, Isaac, and Jacob and the challenge to the Jew in every generation.

Jesus Christ is the God of Abraham, Isaac, and Jacob. To deny Him signifies rejection of the spiritual heritage of the Jewish people and constitutes the underlying cause of many catastrophes in Jewish history. The solution resides in appropriating their own heritage through the work of Christ on the cross.

No one, especially the believer in the Lord Jesus Christ, should ever participate in anti-Semitism. The believer must understand the historical and future plan of God for Israel. Keeping the divine

---

8. *New York Times*, 2 March 1990.

9. *New York Times*, 20 January 1990.

perspective in mind guards against any form of anti-Semitism.[10] The assimilation of divine perspective comes from hearing and believing the message of the Bible. For this reason, I find it imperative to revise and republish this biblical view of anti-Semitism.

BEFORE YOU BEGIN YOUR BIBLE STUDY, be sure that, as a believer in the Lord Jesus Christ, you have named your known sins privately to God (1 John 1:9). You will then be in fellowship with God, under the control of the indwelling Holy Spirit, and ready to learn doctrine from the Word of God.

If you are an unbeliever, the issue is not naming your sins. The issue is faith in Christ:

> He who believes in the Son has eternal life; but he who does not obey [the command to believe in] the Son shall not see life, but the wrath of God abides on him. (John 3:36)

---

10. See R. B. Thieme, Jr., *The Divine Outline of History: Dispensations and the Church* (Houston: R. B. Thieme, Jr., Bible Ministries, 1989), pp. 27–37, 72–79. Hereafter cross-references to my books will cite only title, date of publication (in the first reference), and page(s).

1

The Middle East Crucible

FOCUS ON THE MIDDLE EAST

IN DECEMBER 1987, the eyes of the world focused again on the troubled Middle East, where the smoldering hatred of Palestinian Arabs for their Jewish half-brothers erupted into full-scale rebellion. The Palestinians are demanding an independent and separate state. The ultimate goal of the Palestinian organizations coincides with the designs of their Arab sponsors. The objective is to eliminate the Jewish state and establish an Arab nation in its place.[11]

The very existence of Israel has been a constant source of irritation to the Arabs. The series of defeats the Arabs have suffered since 1948 festers and demands revenge—a final settlement of the dispute. The Palestinian revolt is a new tactic in that ongoing conflict. Through maximum media exposure the Arabs hope to demonstrate that the Jews are the oppressors, the source of Middle East strife, a thorn in the side of the world.

---

11. Lewis, *Semites & Anti-Semites*, 18.

As the flames of war flicker and threaten to spread, the United States seeks a peaceful settlement between these two historical adversaries. Americans, easily deceived by peace overtures, believe—because we desperately wish to believe—that this time some treaty will be binding. Yet we should learn from experience that the signing of peace treaties does not guarantee an end to war. We fail to realize that the antagonisms of the Middle East are intensely focused, with the Arabs dedicated to driving Israel into the sea. Arab overtures of peace will continue only as long as this objective is advanced.

The lure of oil, the enormous untapped mineral assets, and the strategic importance of the Middle East have also enticed the Soviet Union into the strife-torn region. Soviet communism has cultivated Arab client nations for decades. Soviet objectives to acquire access to vast Middle Eastern resources and manipulate the politics of the region would not only supply their own industry with raw material but would leave the oil-dependent Western democracies in desperate straits.

Compounding the peril, the Arabs are prime customers of the Soviet's third largest export industry—military arms. They owe Moscow billions from past deals and could become the source for billions more in the future.[12] Considering current Soviet political and economic woes, the Soviet-Arab relationship is crucial to Moscow. This entente aligns the Soviets against Israel.

At the same time, Islamic nations of the Middle East have a long-standing paranoia of encroachment upon their territory by Israel. With the regional development of chemical and biological weapons, nuclear weapons, and long-range missiles that can strike even the Soviet Union, tension has escalated. The mix of severe instability and weapons of mass destruction point to a future cataclysm that could easily involve both the Soviet Union and the United States.[13]

The balance of power in the Middle East and the ever illusive "peace in our time" hinge on the fate of Israel, that tiny nation

---

12. Danielle Pletka, "Exodus A Godsend for Israel," *Insight* 6 (21 May 1990): 21.
13. *Ibid.*, 21.

of determined people. At least this much can be said for the United States of America: Thus far, we have supplied Israel with aid and overtly supported her cause. But that friendship could erode as we become entangled with issues at home. Beset by political scandals and economic crises, besieged with ultimatums from malcontents, pressured to reduce our military force, will our leadership reflect the moral courage and integrity to continue to back Israel?

Despite a growing euphoria over diminishing Soviet-American tension in the world, the threat of war persists. Probing questions arise over the continuing impasse. Would another Middle East war force the "Big Powers" into a major confrontation, possibly igniting World War III? Will the Israelis be able to hold out and assert themselves against a numerically stronger, better equipped enemy? Would the need for oil force pro-Israeli nations into the Arab camp? Will a negotiated settlement work now, when it has failed in the past? Will the Middle East remain a potential powder keg, ready to blow up at the slightest provocation? Will increasing conflict prompt an intensified thrust of anti-Semitism? Can the Middle East problem be solved? If so, how? Let us consider these questions and determine some of the answers from the biblical point of view.

BIBLICAL PERSPECTIVES ON
THE MIDDLE EAST CRISIS

We live in unpredictable times, on the edge of a precipice. There is instability abroad and at home. The news, which breaks with feverish rapidity, is often gloomy or misinterpreted. But we need not despair. Even though the circumstances of history shift constantly, the One who controls history—the Lord Jesus Christ—is the "same yesterday, and today, yes and forever" (Heb. 13:8).

There is no instability with God (James 1:17). His plan is perfect from its inception to its conclusion. That plan unfolds as a sequence of divine administrations called dispensations.[14] Since

---

14. A dispensation is a period in human history defined in terms of divine revelation. See *The Divine Outline of History*, 3–6.

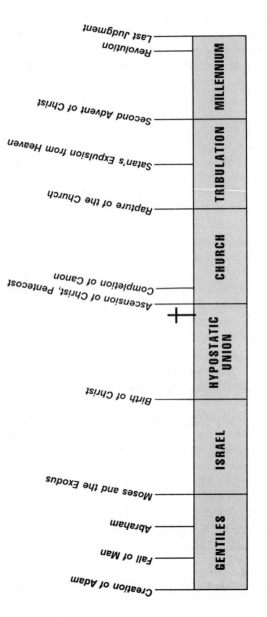

The Divine Outline of History

GENTILES | ISRAEL | HYPOSTATIC UNION | CHURCH | TRIBULATION | MILLENNIUM

Creation of Adam
Fall of Man
Abraham
Moses and the Exodus
Birth of Christ
Ascension of Christ, Pentecost
Completion of Canon
Rapture of the Church
Satan's Expulsion from Heaven
Second Advent of Christ
Revolution
Last Judgment

God has revealed to us in His Word information pertinent to each dispensation, we can determine what the near and distant future impact will be on world events (Deut. 29:29). The dispensational interpretation of Scripture is the key to the correct understanding of current and future conflicts in the Middle East and the role of the Jew in world history.

THE FUTURE CRISIS IN THE MIDDLE EAST

The Bible so clearly defines the Middle East hostilities of the future as to rule out all conjecture. But the Christian simply cannot superimpose future conflicts on the present situation and assume that prophecy is being fulfilled before his eyes. The Church Age is an era when there is no biblical prophecy to be fulfilled.[15]

The next prophetic event will be the Rapture or the removal of the Church from the earth (1 Cor. 15:51–55; Phil. 3:21; 1 Thess. 1:10; Rev. 3:10). The Rapture includes the resurrection of all believers who have died during the Church Age. Then those believers who are alive at that time will be caught up with the newly resurrected believers to meet Christ in the air (1 Thess. 4:13–18). The Rapture terminates the Church Age and initiates the Tribulation.[16]

Unfortunately, tumultuous world conditions encourage distortions of prophecy. Any similarities between current circumstances and Tribulational events incite a glut of speculation. The presence of a recognized Jewish state in Palestine and the alignment of nations as foretold in Daniel 7 and 11 and Revelation 13, 16, and 17 do not signify that we are now experiencing the Tribulation or

---

15. *Ibid.*, 135–38.

16. The Tribulation, also called the "time of Jacob's distress" (Jer. 30:7) and Daniel's seventieth week (Dan. 9:24–27), is a period of seven literal years which complete the Age of Israel. It is prophesied in the Old Testament (Isa. 34:1–6; 63:1–6; Ezek. 38—39; Dan. 11:40–45; Zech. 12 and 14), in the Olivet Discourse of Jesus Christ (Matt. 24—25), and in Revelation 6—19. Old Testament saints will be resurrected at the Second Advent of Christ immediately following the Tribulation (Dan. 12:2, 11–13). *Ibid.*, 72–76.

witnessing the beginning of the Armageddon Campaign. This
future military campaign will actually occur at the end of the
Tribulation as Christ returns to join in the last battle and deliver
the Jews.[17]

Regardless of how long the present (Church) age continues, we
can expect further periodic outbreaks of hostilities, not only in the
Middle East but also in other parts of the world. Jesus Christ
warned of wars and rumors of wars until He returns (Matt 24:6).
In spite of these persistent conflicts in the world His immutable
promise of a future return assures that human history will complete the full dispensational course.

The present Middle East crisis is but one of those wars the Lord
referred to in Matthew. Just as certainly the push to eradicate the
Jews will persist. Satan has sponsored antagonism toward the Jews
throughout history, the current age being no exception. However,
Satan will initiate a period of unparalleled anti-Semitism in the
Tribulation (Rev. 12:17). His all-out effort will culminate in that
future day when four major power blocs will converge on Israel in
an attempt to utterly annihilate the Jews. Satan reasons that if no
Jews survive, God's character will be impugned because His
covenant Word to Israel is proven false.[18]

To understand the scenario for that future conflagration in the
Middle East, we must know the essence of prophecy concerning
the resumption and course of events in the final seven years of the
Jewish dispensation. Two important factors will herald the begin-
ning of the Tribulation and accelerate Satan's offensive against the
Jews.

1. The removal of all believers from the earth at the Rapture of
the Church (1 Thess. 4:13–18).

---

17. *Ibid.*, 75.

18. The unconditional covenants are an everlasting treaty into which God entered
with Abraham and his born-again progeny (Gen. 17:7). The treaty consists of four
separate paragraphs and guarantees the Jews a future, a purpose, and a title deed
to a land of their own. Unconditional in nature, the treaty depends solely upon the
character of God for fulfillment. For an explanation of the four paragraphs given
to Abraham and his progeny see pages 133–34, below.

2. The removal of the restraining ministry of the Holy Spirit (2 Thess. 2:6–7).

After the Rapture the Tribulation commences with three-and-a-half years of power politics in which four major spheres of influence will vie for world domination. Palestine will be at the vortex of the struggle. Keep in mind that no matter what political situation may exist, all directions in the Bible are given in their relationship to Palestine.

Paralleling this power struggle unprecedented evangelism will be conducted by one hundred forty-four thousand Jewish evangelists whom God will seal and protect against the anti-Semitic element during the entire Tribulation (Rev. 7:4–10). But in the last three-and-a-half years of the Tribulation anti-Semitism and general alienation toward the Jews will become so intense that the period is called the "Great Tribulation" (Matt. 24:21–22; Rev. 7:14; 12:17).

Early in the first half of the Tribulation a ten nation federation will be arrayed in the west with headquarters at Rome.[19] An improbable alliance between the gentile dictator of the Revived Roman Empire and "the false prophet" (Rev. 19:20; 20:10), the Jewish dictator of Palestine, will be consummated (Dan. 11:36–39). By the middle of the Tribulation the statue of the Roman dictator ("abomination of desolation," Dan. 12:11) will be erected in the restored temple at Jerusalem.

The three remaining spheres of influence in this apocalyptic drama will not languish idly and allow their expectations for power to vanish. They plan an offensive against the King of the West and the dictator of Palestine. This war of wars will be launched by a

---

19. The ten nation federation or "ten horns" of Daniel 7:7–8, 23–24, Revelation 13:1–10 and 17:8–10, is sometimes called the Revived Roman Empire. This kingdom is related to the Roman Empire by Daniel's vision of the "great statue" (Dan. 2:31–45). The five major divisions of the statue represent five great gentile kingdoms beginning with Nebuchadnezzar's Babylon (Dan. 2:38). The fifth kingdom, "the feet and toes of iron and clay," is a future extension of the fourth kingdom, "the legs of iron," the Roman Empire. The ruler of this federation (the King of the West) is referred to as "the beast" (Rev. 13:1–2), the "little horn" (Dan. 7:8), the "prince that shall come" (Dan. 9:26–27), the "god of fortresses" (Dan. 11:38), the "man of lawlessness" (2 Thess. 2:3–10), and the "scarlet beast" (Rev. 17:3).

simultaneous attack from the King of the South and the King of the North (Dan. 11; cf., Ezek. 38—39). These forces will be counterattacked by the King of the West and the Kings of the East (Dan. 11:44; Rev. 16:12). But this final conflict cannot transpire until after the Rapture of the Church.

THE CURRENT CRISIS IN THE MIDDLE EAST

Should the Rapture occur in the foreseeable future, then what we are now observing in the Middle East is but the setting of the stage, the dress rehearsal for the final curtain of Middle East conflicts. Under these circumstances, the King of the North would indeed be the Soviet Union, and the King of the South would be the united Arab states. The King of the West would be a federation of European states and the Kings of the East (the kings of "the rising of the sun," literal translation of the term in Revelation 16:12) would be represented by the Chinese communists and their allies. Mentioned prophetically in Scripture, each power sphere of the Tribulation is intensely concentrated on the Middle East in general and on Israel in particular. Each will be guilty of anti-Semitism.

Humanly speaking, why should such a small nation with a people so few in number, who wish only to be left in peace, cause such animosity among her neighbors, as well as create such sensational controversy among the nations of the world? One reason comes from the natural realm. Abraham is the father both of the Jewish race through Isaac and of the Arab race through Ishmael. His progeny through Ishmael are the traditional enemies of the Jews (Gen. 16:11–12). The principle still exists that "Hagar's son"—the son of Sarah's slave girl—always persecutes the "son of the freeborn"—Sarah's son, Isaac, who was born by a miracle of God's grace (Gal. 4:23, 29; cf., 2 Tim. 3:12). The enmity between the two peoples is illustrated by the Arab claim to the territory deeded by God to the descendants of Isaac's line.

The second reason for animosity toward the Jews comes from the spiritual realm. The angelic conflict, that unseen warfare that continues between God and Satan, involves Israel as a focal point.[20]

Although the Arabs may find it expedient to pen their names to any number of peace pacts with the Jews, like the devil who sponsors anti-Semitism, they will only depart "until an opportune time" (Luke 4:13*b*) to await a more favorable advantage for attack. The Jews know this and maintain constant vigilance.

But suppose the Arabs in a concerted effort were able to destroy the Jewish state. They would gain little from dividing up that small strip of arid real estate. Why, then, are they so intent on Israel's destruction? The Bible resolves this intriguing question by describing satanic strategy against the Jews and by clearly demonstrating that *no· one tampers with the Jews without terrible consequences*. To their own detriment this is a lesson that many a nation and many an individual have yet to learn.

God made a solemn promise that Jews will always remain on the earth. If He will preserve them in the Tribulation, the bleakest hour of their history, He will never abandon them now. "For the Lord will not abandon His people [the Jews] on account of His great name" (1 Sam. 12:22*a*).

Superficially, all Middle East crises can be attributed to historical events; but below the surface a more sinister reason prevails—the satanic influence on history.[21] There is an evil that permeates not only the Middle East but the entire world. Without understanding the nature of that evil and the extent of its pernicious outreach, you will never unravel the complexities of historical trends. Nor will you realize why the Jews have been singled out as the object of hatred, the universal scapegoat. Nor why the Jews, more than any other race, have experienced man's inhumanity to man, or why anti-Semitism exists at all.

---

20. For an explanation of the angelic conflict and how it affects Israel, see Chapter 2 and Chapter 5, below.

21. See *Demonism* (1974), 9–17.

2

The Source of Anti-Semitism

Anti-Semitism Defined

Anti-semitism is opposition to, prejudice against, or intolerance of the Jewish people. However, the term Semite encompasses much more than just the Jews. Jews are but one branch of the Semitic peoples, which include the ancient Assyrians, Midianites, Chaldeans, Moabites, Edomites, Ammonites, as well as the present Arabs, Syrians, Armenians, a considerable portion of the people of Ethiopia, and of the Middle East in general. To be accurate, therefore, anti-Semitism should be defined as opposition to *all* Semites.

Yet such is not the case. Jews alone are the target for anti-Semitism, which may run the gamut from antipathy to violent hatred. Since most people understand anti-Semitism to be the terrible evil of anti-Jewish sentiment and action which has plagued history, I will continue to use the word in the dictionary sense to refer only to the Jews.

HISTORICAL PERSPECTIVES OF ANTI-SEMITISM

The venom that renders masses of people susceptible to anti-Jewish agitation is more than fear, distrust, prejudice, insecurity, or envy. This vicious hatred reflects the angelic conflict and Satan's subsequent machinations to defeat the plan of God.[22] No matter how nonspiritual he may be, the Jew is the center of a very real spiritual warfare.

THE ANGELIC CONFLICT

The angelic conflict originated before man existed on the earth. This great warfare began when Lucifer, the anointed cherub, the highest of all angelic creatures, challenged divine authority and revolted against God (Isa. 14:13–14; Ezek. 28:12–15). By divine judgment, Lucifer was removed from his exalted position and sentenced to eternal condemnation, with the sentence to be executed in the future (Isa. 14:15; cf., Matt. 25:41).

If shock can be experienced in heaven, the angels must have been stunned at the news of Lucifer's fall. To think that angelic volition could be expressed in rejection of grace! For all eternity the lines were drawn which would divide the angels into two groups—elect and fallen. What began in the arrogant mind of Lucifer had erupted into overt angelic revolution. Lucifer became the adversary of God and successfully persuaded one-third of the angelic host to ally themselves with him in defiance of God (Rev. 12:4). Thus, with Satan as the central antagonist, the angelic conflict raged throughout the universe.

Human history is both the extension and resolution of this heavenly conflict. Mankind was created to duplicate the conditions of that prehistoric revolt.[23] Like the angels, humanity was endowed with free will and that free will would be tested to see whether

---

22. The angelic conflict refers to prehistoric angelic opposition to God (2 Pet. 2:4; Jude 6) that continues as spiritual warfare in human history (1 Pet. 5:8; cf., Eph. 6:10–17).

23. See *Christian Integrity* (1990), 66–68.

man would choose for or against God. Therefore, man came under the close scrutiny of both the elect and the fallen angels (Job 2:1–3; Luke 15:7, 10).

Satan himself instigated the events that led to man's Fall. Adam followed the same pattern of arrogance which initiated the angelic revolution. But Satan had not counted on the grace of God providing salvation long before the need arose (1 Pet. 1:18–20). God did not desert man just because he had failed the volitional test in the garden of Eden (Gen. 2:16–17). After the Fall He would test man again in the state of sinfulness by offering salvation through faith in the coming Savior. Satan was present when God enucleated Genesis 3:15.

> And I [God] will put enmity between you [Satan] and the woman, and between your seed [unbelieving humanity] and her seed [the virgin-born Messiah]; He [the Seed] shall bruise you on the head [Satan's final doom], and you [Satan] shall bruise Him [Messiah] on the heel [a reference to the cross]. (Gen. 3:15)[24]

Although detailed information concerning the person and the work of the Savior would be revealed progressively, Satan instantly understood the identity of the Seed of the woman. The arrival of the Savior would settle the angelic conflict in God's favor. To prevent God's plan from unfolding, Satan (the fallen Lucifer) designed a counter strategy. As a result, the devil motivated the first recorded murder in human history (Gen. 4:8; cf., 1 John 3:12) in an effort to eliminate the regenerate line through which Messiah would come.

Cain's murder of Abel set a precedent fraught with the danger of triggering a feud of personal vengeance. God would use the law, as it existed in antediluvian times, to keep the human race from self-destruction. He personally pronounced Cain's punishment (Gen. 4:9–15). Cain was barred from farming, the vocation he

---

24. Scriptures cited in this book are from the New American Standard Bible (NASB). Bracketed commentary further explains the quotation or reflects exegesis from Bible class lectures. Tape recordings of Bible classes are available on request from R. B. Thieme, Jr., Bible Ministries, Houston, Texas.

loved, and was condemned to be "a vagrant and wanderer on the earth."

Furthermore, God reestablished the Savior's line in the birth of Seth (Gen. 4:25). But Satan never gives up. He struck again in an attempt to corrupt the entire human race to make it impossible for the Savior to be born. The attack of the angelic infiltration of the human race is recorded in Genesis 6.[25] God's counterattack was the flood, which covered the earth and destroyed the *Nephilim*, preserving only Noah and his family.

All this occurred long before a Jewish race existed. However, from the sons of Noah God chose one branch of the family, the descendants of Shem, to represent Him on earth and be custodians of His holy Word (Rom. 3:2). Through the line of Shem Messiah would come (2 Sam. 7:8, 12; cf., John 4:22; Rom. 9:5). Satan then concentrated on one man—Abraham; on one family—Jacob's; on one nation—Israel; on one race—the Jews.

THE ORIGIN OF THE JEWS

The Jewish race is unique in all history. God formed this people for the specific purpose of being His instruments for the development and dissemination of His Word. As Israel's founder, God selected a man of pure Chaldean extraction. His name was Abram, and he was the ninth in line from Shem. Semitic Abram was a Gentile, just as the Arabs today are Semitic but Gentile.

In those days long past there was no division of the earth's population into Gentiles and Jews. Such a dichotomy occurred later when Abram (renamed Abraham by God, in Gen. 17:5) was circumcised at the age of ninety-nine to become the father of the Jewish race. Until then there were only Gentiles of Hamitic, Semitic, and Japhetic origin—but no Jews.

---

25. The intermarriage of fallen angels, "sons of God" (Gen. 6:2), and "the daughters of men" produced a super race, *"Nephilim"* (v. 4). Eventually, if left to continue, the cohabiting fallen angels would have entirely reduced the human race to part angel–part man, a corruption that would have made the advent of Messiah impossible. See *Victorious Proclamation* (1977), 6–9.

Abram lived in Ur of the Chaldees (southern Babylonia) under a system of decadent culture and totalitarian paganism. Convinced of the existence of God, he came to know and believe in the Savior as He was then revealed (Gen. 15:6). Because it was imperative that he be separated from his background and surroundings of idolatry, the Lord said to Abram:

> "Go forth from your country, and from your relatives and from your father's house, to the land which I will show you." (Gen. 12:1)

To that command of separation, God added five distinct promises. These are listed in Genesis 12:

1. "I will make you a great nation" (v. 2).

2. "I will bless you" (v. 2).

3. "And make your name great" (v. 2).

4. "And so you shall be a blessing" (v. 2).

5. "In you [a Messianic reference] all the families of the earth shall be blessed" (v. 3).

It is doubtful that Abram realized the full extent of God's promise concerning himself and his progeny since prophecy often has a near and far fulfillment. But clearly, the first prophetic promise God made to Abram revealed the founder and foundation of the Jewish race and augured great national blessings for the future. The second promise provided personal blessings for the patriarch, particularly once he reached spiritual maturity. The next two promises indicated the very structure of Abraham's life, and the last paragraph concerned the Seed of Abraham—Jesus Christ (Gal. 3:8–9, 16).

From time to time God would reiterate and amplify the various paragraphs of the everlasting treaty which He had made with Abraham and his progeny, a treaty which is called the Abrahamic Covenant.[26] The covenant guarantees the new race a future, a purpose, and a title deed to a land of their own.

---

26. The other unconditional covenants are essentially reiterations of the Abrahamic Covenant. See footnote 18, page 6, above.

Bear in mind that descent from Abraham does not automatically qualify one as a recipient of the unconditional covenants.

> For they are not all Israel who are descended from Israel; neither are they all children because they are Abraham's descendants, but: "Through Isaac your descendants will be named." That is, it is not the children of the flesh who are children of God, but the children of the promise are regarded as descendants. (Rom. 9:6*b*–8)

Both Jacob and Esau were grandsons of Abraham, but God did not look on them with equal favor. "Jacob I loved, but Esau I hated" (Rom. 9:13*b*; cf., Mal. 1:2–3). Jacob received the blessing because he was regenerate, a child of God through spiritual birth.[27] Clearly, Jewish ancestry was not the only criterion for transmission of the divine promises on which Israel was founded. The spiritual birth of the physical progeny of Abraham was essential for gaining access to the divine promises.

Therefore, the real foundation of the Jewish race is regeneration. Abraham was born again (Rom. 4:1–5; cf., John 3:3–7, 16). He exhibited faith in the promise of God and God gave to Abraham what he could never merit on his own. Isaac and Jacob also believed, Esau did not. In the formation of true Israel the racial Jew must become the regenerate Jew.

THE CLAUSE CONDEMNING ANTI-SEMITISM

If Abraham failed to grasp the full significance of God's prophetic declaration, Satan did not, and he plotted accordingly. Since God was intent on establishing and blessing the Abrahamic line, then Satan had to attempt to destroy that line.

To countermand Satan's evil design against the promised new race, God affixed a blessing and cursing clause to the Abrahamic

---

27. Spiritual birth designates the judicial imputation of eternal life that occurs by grace through faith in the person of the Messiah, Jesus Christ. Abraham (Gen. 15:6) and Nicodemus (John 3:1–16) are clear examples of men who are "born again."

Covenant. The clause vouched for sustained divine provision, protection, and preservation of Jews in every generation. God had served notice that the Jew *will* survive human history.

Unlike the first two paragraphs of the Abrahamic Covenant, the anti-Semitism clause applies fully to the unregenerate as well as the regenerate Jew. The race must endure to enter the Tribulation. This is that future time in which all believers of the Church are removed and God is again dealing with Israel as a nation. Unregenerate Jews who subsequently accept Christ as Savior during that seven-year period (Zech. 12:10—13:9) will constitute the final remnant. They will participate in the complete fulfillment of the unconditional covenants when Christ returns at the end of the Tribulation (Matt. 24:27–31).[28]

The anti-Semitism clause reads:

> And I [God] will bless those who bless you, and the one who curses you I will curse. (Gen. 12:3)

Genesis 12:3 is by no means the only statement of divine approval of pro-Semitism and divine condemnation of anti-Semitism. Other affirmations are given in principle and fulfillment throughout the Bible. To cite but two examples: The Lord blessed the house of Potiphar, the Egyptian, for Joseph's sake (Gen. 39:5) but judged Egypt for enslaving the Jews (Gen. 15:13–14). While He prospered Cyrus, King of Persia, for his attitude toward captive Judah (Ezra 1:1–4), God executed wicked Haman and all who sought to exterminate the Jews during the reign of Xerxes (Esth. 3:5–6, 13; 6:10—9:15).

Thus, a correlation exists between the rise and fall of individuals, nations, and empires and their attitude toward the Jew. The clause first presented in Genesis 12:3 serves as a warning not only to Satan and his demonic hordes but to all mankind. God will bless all who bless the Jews and punish all who seek their destruction.

---

28. Christ returns to deliver the Jews (Isa. 10:20–23; 11:11–16; 14:1–3; Joel 2:16—3:21; Zech. 10:6–12) and to establish His kingdom which is called the Millennium (Ps. 72; Isa. 11, 35, 62, 65; Zech. 14:4–9; Rev. 20). See *The Divine Outline of History*, 75–79.

The blessing and cursing clause also has implications for the Jewish race in the future. The principle is stated in Hebrews.

> For those whom the Lord loves He disciplines, and He scourges [skins alive with a whip] every son whom He receives. (Heb. 12:6; cf., Prov. 3:12)

God's love for the people He had chosen to represent Him on earth during the Age of the Jews remains constant and unchangeable. He keeps His covenant to Israel (Deut. 7:7–9), even if they fail Him.

Divine love is expressed in many ways—in blessing or discipline. When His people fail, God metes out the appropriate punishment. Remember discipline and judgment are a divine prerogative.[29] God reserves the exclusive right to handle His own affairs. Any person or nation who gets between God who holds the whip and the one on whom punishment is about to descend receives the brunt of the lash. Be warned! Stay out of the way of divine discipline especially where the Jews are concerned!

God feels strongly about the Jews—so strongly, in fact, that He refers to them as the "apple [pupil] of His eye" (Deut. 32:10; Ps. 17:8; Prov. 7:2; Zech. 2:8). The pupil is one of the most protected parts of the human anatomy. The frontal bone structure of the face guards the recessed pupil from potential injury; the brows and lashes screen out dust; the eyelids shield the pupil from the harmful glare of light; and the tear ducts wash away smudge and dirt. Likewise, divine intervention protects the Jews from the devastating blows of anti-Semitism. In other words, God Himself ensures that the Jews cannot be abused with impunity.

HISTORICAL RAMIFICATIONS OF ANTI-SEMITISM

The divinely established clause against anti-Semitism remains in force throughout history. God has promised Israel a future as a nation. Thus, He will continue to deliver the Jew until the end of time.

---

29. *Christian Suffering* (1987), 28–53.

Wherever anti-Semitism prevails, the people involved are underwriting their own destruction. No individual or nation ever survives anti-Semitism; they destroy themselves. I will demonstrate in the next two chapters that nations reach their zenith because of their kindly treatment of the Jews, and that equally powerful nations decline because of their persecution of the Jews.

The outworking of this principle is recognized in the *Encyclopaedia Britannica.*

> It is a noteworthy fact of history that great conquerors, Alexander, Caesar, and Napoleon, have always treated the Jews well: they recognized their religious function and sought to give it freedom to develop, for their own advantage as well as that of the Jews. On the other hand, lesser men, endowed with narrower outlooks, have failed to recognize the Jew and have sought to crush him. In their desire to impose an artificial uniformity, they 'broke down the boundaries of people and put down the inhabitants' (Isa. 10:13). But such Procrustean methods are contrary to nature, and tyranny, whether towards Jews or towards any others, has never secured permanent results. The same policy of religious unification has characterized subsequent dynasties, from the Assyrians to the Romanovs, and the same fate has overtaken them. The Jew has survived their disappearance.[30]

---

30. *Encyclopaedia Britannica,* 14th ed., s.v. "Jews."

3

Anti-Semitism in Ancient History

THE AMALEKITES

THE JEWS HAVE MET WITH PERSONAL ANTAGONISM since the
founding of the race. But while they experienced oppression on a
grand scale in Egypt, they had yet to encounter anti-Semitism as
a nation. The first instance occurred shortly after the Exodus when
God used Moses to bring the Jews out of Egyptian slavery. The
account is described by these terse words: "Then Amalek came
and fought against Israel at Rephidim" (Ex. 17:8). The attack was
treacherous and completely unprovoked, directed against the
Jewish stragglers—the rear guard—as they journeyed through the
wilderness.

Thought to be the progeny of Esau (Gen. 36:12), the Amalekites
existed in the days of Abraham (Gen. 14:7). Although they figured
prominently in the Old Testament, they have since vanished from
history. Archaeologists, despite a diligent search, have failed to
unearth even a vestige of this ancient people. Why? The
Amalekites hold the dubious honor of being "the first of the

nations" to wage war against the newly chartered Jewish nation (Num. 24:20). The assault guaranteed their doom as God announced, "I will utterly blot out the memory of Amalek from under heaven" (Ex. 17:14b).

The Israelites were to be the appointed executioners of the Amalekites (Deut. 25:17–19; 1 Sam. 15:3, 18), but God knew they would fail to carry out His sentence (1 Sam. 28:18–19). How much suffering and oppression the Jews could have spared themselves had they obeyed God's mandate promptly and completely! But since Amalek would continue to be Israel's bitter foe, God swore that "the Lord will have war with Amalek from generation to generation" (Ex. 17:16). The Jews would continue to be victimized time and again by Amalekite aggression (Judges 3:12–13; 10:12; 1 Sam. 15:3ff; 30:1).

During the time of the Judges, the Israelites found themselves repeatedly under the heel of the Amalekites. Saul, Israel's first king, sent by God on a mission to annihilate this scourge, was to rue the day he spared Agag, the king of Amalek, as well as the "best" of the spoils (1 Sam. 15:15, 18–19, 26). Saul was set aside for insubordination to God's Word and eventually died the sin unto death (maximum discipline for the believer in time, 1 Chron. 10:13–14). Adding insult to injury, an Amalekite opportunist robbed Saul of his crown and armband, intending to capitalize on his death (2 Sam. 1).

Throughout his reign, David pursued the Amalekites. Yet they were not completely eradicated until the days of Hezekiah (1 Chron. 4:39–43) when the curse of Genesis 12:3 was fulfilled to the letter. God never goes back on His Word.

BALAAM'S CURSE ON ISRAEL

That God keeps His word was precisely what Balaam had in mind when he stood on the mountaintop and pronounced blessing instead of cursing on Israel:

> God is not a man, that He should lie, nor a son of man, that He should repent; Has He said, and will He not do it? Or has He spoken, and will He not make it good?

> Behold, I have received a command to bless; when He
> has blessed, then I cannot revoke it. (Num. 23:19–20)

The man who spoke these words was famed for his divinations and imprecations. Indeed, his name meant "destroyer of the people." Though he knew the Lord (Num. 22:8, 13, 19, 38), he lived in a state of reversionism[31] and, if the price was right, he could be persuaded to dabble in wizardry, regardless of God's prohibition.

The price was right when Balak, the king of the Moabites, sent for Balaam to cast a spell on the approaching Israelites (Num. 22:17). But try as he might, Balaam had not been able to pronounce the curse. God restrained him (Num. 22:12). Instead, Balaam explained to the frustrated king:

> How shall I curse, whom God has not cursed? And how
> can I denounce, whom the Lord has not denounced?
> (Num. 23:8).

Balaam was convinced that further enchantments against the Jews would be useless and displeasing to God (Num. 24:1). His attitude indicates that he had acknowledged his sins (Ps. 32:5). Once back in fellowship with God, the future of Israel was opened before his eyes (Num. 24:3–9, 15–19, 21–24). Inspired by the Holy Spirit, Balaam shouted a reiteration of the anti-Semitism clause of the Abrahamic Covenant:

> Blessed is everyone who blesses you [Israel], and cursed
> is everyone who curses you. (Num. 24:9b)

When Balaam's vision ended he faced a furious Balak. Balaam now realized that the wealth, honor, and promotion promised by the Moabite king had slipped through his fingers. What had he done? He had ruined his career for the sake of those Jews.

Materialism lust and power lust had overwhelmed Balaam

---

31. Reversionism is recession from any stage of spiritual growth through carnality (perpetuating unconfessed sin in the life) or negative volition to God's Word. Reversionism does not imply loss of salvation. For more information you may request tape-recorded lessons available from R. B. Thieme, Jr., Bible Ministries, Houston, Texas. See also *Demonism* (1974), 84–89.

(2 Pet. 2:15; Jude 11). Maybe there was some way he could extricate himself and still come out ahead. He had an idea: If the Jews could be lured into fornicating with the women of Midian, they would bring on their own cursing. Balaam's advice was followed (Rev. 2:14). As a result, twenty-four thousand Israelites succumbed to the temptation. They came under the sin unto death and perished (Num. 25:9).

As for Balaam, in bringing about the curse in an indirect manner, he placed himself in direct line for punishment. When God's judgment struck the Midianites, Balaam was slain with the sword (Num. 31:8). He had foreseen the doom of those who would curse Israel. His involvement brought him under the same curse.

THE ASSYRIANS

Another classic example of anti-Semitism is the case of the Assyrians. One of the greatest empires in the ancient world, Assyria possessed every ingredient essential for maintaining a vigorous and powerful supremacy. Yet Assyria was completely humbled at the height of glory.

THE RISE OF ASSYRIA

The most striking feature of Assyria was military power. A series of victories expanded the borders of the empire, extending Assyrian hegemony over much of the known world. The superbly trained Assyrian army remained undefeated for two hundred years. Egypt was neutralized and the Hittites conquered. With the assimilation of their embryonic iron industry, Assyria was able to compete with the Phoenicians for the monopoly of the iron market. Assyria became a leading smelter and distributor of iron implements and weapons for the ancient world.

But Assyrians could boast of more than military success. The combination of a system of free enterprise and profitable trading markets created thriving commerce and a dynamic economy.

Over the decades, the names of Tiglath-Pileser III, Shalmaneser V, Sargon, Sennacherib, and Esar-Haddon were synonymous with conquest and cruelty. Their names struck a chord of fear and awe throughout the ancient world. Yet, not until the reign of Esar-Haddon's son, Assur-bani-pal, did Assyria reach the peak of splendor, luxury, and decadence that foreshadowed the approaching disintegration of the empire.

The decline of this great empire was inevitable for a number of reasons. The Assyrians had begun to consider themselves invincible. They abused their strength. Impressed with their indisputable magnificence and wealth, they succumbed to apostasy.

As if that were not enough, the Assyrians—themselves a Semitic people—embarked on a policy of anti-Semitism. That alone would lead to disaster (Gen. 12:3; cf., Isa. 33:1–4). True, they recovered briefly as a result of Jonah's ministry in 754 B.C. when Nineveh, the Assyrian capital, experienced a tremendous spiritual awakening and conversion (Jonah 3:8–10). Divine judgment was temporarily averted.

In the following nine critical years under a decadent monarchy, a pivotal group of believers positive to God's Word held the nation together. The turning point came in 745 B.C., when an unknown palace gardener usurped the throne and assumed the royal name of Tiglath-Pileser III.

During his reign (745–727 B.C.), Assyria was once again in ascendancy. By his genius, despite occasional ruthlessness, Tiglath-Pileser established a stable governmental structure not only in Assyria but also in conquered territories. But his masterful rule would not last.

By 739 B.C. the Assyrian armies threatened Judah. Subsequently, a policy of anti-Semitism persisted in one form or another—from exacting tribute to demanding exorbitant bribes, from deportations of hostages to outright conquest and plunder.

History records that Assyria's constant warfare eventually ruined the economy. Financing unnecessary military campaigns, extravagant expenditures on royal pleasures and superfluous building programs finally depleted the empire's resources. These excesses contributed to a rapid decline, but the predominant reason for the Assyrian downfall was anti-Semitism.

THE FALL OF ASSYRIA

The Bible reports how God dealt a deadly blow to Assyrian anti-Semitism in the reign of King Hezekiah (701 B.C.). Assyria had again invaded Judah and Jerusalem was next on the agenda for conquest. In an awesome display of power and armed might the army of the Assyrian empire massed outside the city walls and rattled its collective sabers.

The Rabshakeh, commander in chief of the army, arrogantly demanded the unconditional surrender of Jerusalem. Concurrently, he blasted the population with pernicious propaganda and blatantly challenged the God of Israel. Isaiah records his taunts.

> "Who among all the gods of these lands [already conquered] have delivered their land from my hand, that the Lord should deliver Jerusalem from my hand?" (Isa. 36:20).

If the Rabshakeh expected the white flag of surrender to be raised, he was in for a disappointment. Isaiah's faithful teaching of God's Word made the difference. The believing remnant fearlessly stood their ground and answered the challenge with unflinching silence (Isa. 36:21). These believers remained courageous in spite of the defeatist attitude of their leaders (Isa. 37:1–3). They firmly believed that God would deliver them and His city.

Little did the Rabshakeh suspect how soon he would have to swallow his words, nor did Sennacherib, the king, realize that he had sealed his own doom by pursuing a path of anti-Semitism. God was already in the process of honoring His Word and the faith of His people. A divine communique was dispatched to the king of Judah via the prophet Isaiah: God would personally intervene for the Jews (Isa. 10:12; cf., 37:6–7, 28–29, 33–35). The reckoning came at dawn, shortly before the troops were to muster for roll call:

> Then the angel of the Lord went out, and struck 185,000 in the camp of the Assyrians; and when men [the Israelites] arose early in the morning, behold, all of them [the Assyrians] were dead bodies. (Isa. 37:36)

A sweeping pictorial account of this spectacular event was captured by the great baroque painter, Peter Paul Rubens (1577–1640), who depicted with some artistic license the last gasp of Assyrian might in his epic masterpiece, *The Defeat of Sennacherib*. With his army decimated by the Lord Himself, Sennacherib was forced to retreat in humiliation to Nineveh (2 Chron. 32:21; Isa. 37:37). Shortly thereafter, true to Isaiah's prophecy, he was murdered by two of his sons while engaged in idolatry (Isa. 37:38). Still, Assyria failed to heed the warning. A continuing course of anti-Semitism paralleled the steady decline of the empire.

The end came in 612 B.C. with startling suddenness. Cyaxares, the king of the Medes, and Nabopolassar, then ruler of Babylon, joined forces with the Scythians to take Nineveh. Launching a surprise attack, the Medes descended from the Iranian Plateau; the Chaldeans came across the Tigris-Euphrates Valley; and out of the north, from the direction of the Caspian Sea, swept the Scythians. The capture of Nineveh marked the total collapse of the empire.

Within three short months, Assyria, which could trace her beginning to the third millennium B.C., ceased to exist. God's Word was vindicated. "Behold, I am against you," the Lord of hosts proclaimed against Assyria, as well as all anti-Semites. The third chapter of the Book of Nahum describes the fall of Nineveh. In fact, so completely did the curse of Genesis 12:3 come to pass that no trace of the Assyrians remains to this day. But the Jews survive!

This amazing fact of secular history, entwined with divine revelation, is documented in *The Cambridge Ancient History*.

> The disappearance of the Assyrian people will always remain an unique and striking phenomenon in ancient history. Other, similar, kingdoms and empires have indeed passed away, but the people have lived on. Recent discoveries have, it is true, shown that poverty-stricken communities perpetuated the old Assyrian names at various places, for instance on the ruined site of Ashur, for many centuries, but the essential truth remains the same. A nation which had existed two

thousand years and had ruled a wide area, lost its
independent character. To account for this two considerations may be urged. First, even in lands where, as
Gibbon has remarked, the people are of a libidinous
complexion, the Assyrians seem to have been unduly
devoted to practices which can only end in racial suicide
. . . No other land seems to have been sacked and
pillaged so completely as was Assyria; no other people,
unless it be Israel, was ever so completely enslaved.

In another way the fall of Assyria is unique, in that
after centuries of military domination in Mesopotamia,
and after decades of imperial power, it is almost
impossible for the modern historian surely to trace any
lasting Assyrian influence on the history of succeeding
ages.[32]

Syria, Phoenicia, Philistia

At a time when the Jews were completing the reconstruction of
the Temple in Jerusalem, the "crushing weight of judgment" was
prophesied by Zechariah in 518 b.c. against three anti-Semitic
nations. The Jews had encountered vicious opposition during their
first attempt to rebuild this sacred place that would embody and
represent their whole realm of theology.

Discouragement, constant intimidation, misrepresentation of the
facts to the Persian monarch, Artaxerxes, had disrupted the
building program for fourteen years (Ezra 4:11–24). Then God
raised up Zechariah who prophesied that God would preserve the
remnant of His people from the gentile oppression that threatened
their extinction. The message was one of confidence in the
deliverance of the Lord. Construction resumed and the Temple
was finished in 516 b.c.

From 516 to 323 b.c., the Jews would enjoy their "golden age,"
ultimately brought about by maximum dissemination and

---

32. J. B. Bury, S. A. Cook, and F. E. Adcock, ed., *The Cambridge Ancient History*,
10 vols. (Cambridge: The University Press, 1965), 3:130–31.

perception of Bible doctrine, and obedience to God's Word. Such prosperity, however, would arouse envy among the Syrians, Phoenicians, and Philistines who were all potentially anti-Semitic. Zechariah foretold how one hundred and eighty years later these anti-Semitic nations would be obliterated (Zech. 9:1ff).

THE SYRIANS

Another branch of Semitic people, the Syrians, descended from Shem's youngest son Aram (Gen. 10:22), brought God's judgment upon themselves by their hostile attitude toward the Jews. Zechariah's prophecy would affect three city-states in Syria: Hadrach, Damascus, and Hamath.

> The burden [a crushing weight of judgment] of the word of the Lord is against the land of Hadrach, with Damascus as its resting place (for the eyes of men, especially of all the tribes of Israel, are toward the Lord), and Hamath also, which borders on it; Tyre and Sidon, though they are very wise. (Zech. 9:1–2)

Hadrach was the northern most city-state. Located on the Orontes, to the south of Hamath and north of Damascus, the land is mentioned in Assyrian monuments under the name Hatarrika. To the south lay Aram-Dammasek, the "Syria of Damascus" of Second Samuel 8:5–6. Damascus owed its economic stability and prominence to the fertile valley of the Abana and to placement along the important trade and military routes of the ancient world. Hamath, bordering on Hadrach and Damascus, was the capital of Upper Syria.

During her turbulent history, Syria engaged in frequent but mostly unsuccessful warfare with Israel and Judah in the days of the monarchy. Syria vied with Egypt over possession and control of the land that God had promised the Jews. As a result animosity between the Jews and Syrians remained deep-rooted. Then, as now, Syria "has planned evil" against Israel, for which punitive action from God is the inevitable result (Isa. 7:5–7).

The crushing weight of judgment Zechariah had predicted smashed Syria in the year 332 B.C., shortly after Alexander the Great soundly routed the army of Persian king Darius III at Issus. Hadrach and Hamath fell prey to the conquering Macedonian army, while Damascus, then the provincial capital of the Persian Empire, capitulated without a struggle. Alexander was now in full command of Syria. In Alexander, the Jews found a staunch ally and admirer. For a time Jewish troubles ceased.

THE PHOENICIANS

The Phoenicians were the Hamitic inhabitants of Tyre, Sidon, and Carthage. They called themselves the Canaanites and were foremost among traders and seafarers, the explorers of antiquity— merchants to the ancient world. But the Phoenicians were also known for their worship of Baal and their practice of the phallic cult.[33] Israel was greatly influenced and severely punished for following Canaanite religious practices at the time of King Ahab (Ahab's wife, Jezebel, was a Sidonian, 1 Kings 16:31–33), as well as during the reign of King Jehoram of Judah.

Tyre exemplifies the Phoenicians. This city was one of the most prominent and perhaps the wealthiest in the ancient world. Strongly fortified, this island municipality was located on the eastern shore of the Mediterranean Sea. Immense walls one hundred and fifty feet high and a hundred feet wide made Tyre a veritable citadel. On top of those walls the Tyrians loved to race their chariots.

PHOENICIAN DECLINE. For trade purposes, Israel established friendly relations with Tyre during David's reign. Apparently these were maintained even in the divided kingdom.[34] Then in 842 B.C.

---

33. The unrestrained abandon to sex in the worship of the generative power in nature as symbolized by the phallus.

34. During the reign of David, all Israelites had been consolidated into a United Monarchy. This status continued until after Solomon's death, when a system of heavy taxation and apostasy disrupted the union of the tribes. The ten northern tribes defected under Jeroboam and formed the Kingdom of Israel. The two

the Philistines and Arabs attacked Judah with disastrous results for the Jews (2 Chron. 21:16–17). This military defeat was divine discipline for Israel's continued association with the phallic cult. Sometimes God must use evil nations to shock His people into awareness of and recovery from their persistent reversionism.

But the Philistines overstepped divine boundaries. In their ingrained hatred for the Jews, they persecuted and oppressed their Jewish captives consigning them to brutal slavery. They embraced a national policy of anti-Semitism.

Then the Phoenicians entered the scene. Motivated by the possibility of further enrichment for themselves, the Phoenicians capitalized on the misfortune of the Jews. After joining the Philistines in the plunder of Jerusalem and Judah, they bought and sold Jewish captives to the Greeks (Ezek. 27:13; cf., Joel 3:4–8). The prophet Joel harshly denounced the Phoenicians for this cruelty and declared God's judgment on them for their anti-Semitism.

> Moreover, what are you to Me, O Tyre, Sidon, and all the regions of Philistia? Are you rendering Me a recompense? But if you do recompense Me, swiftly and speedily I will return your recompense on your head. (Joel 3:4)

Three hundred years before the destruction actually happened, Ezekiel predicted the fall of Tyre with divinely inspired accuracy and detail. The prophecy is found in Ezekiel 26:

> Because Tyre has said concerning Jerusalem, Aha, the gateway of the peoples is broken. . . . I shall be filled, now that she is laid waste, therefore, thus says the Lord God . . . I will bring up many nations against you. . . . And they will destroy the walls of Tyre, and break down her towers; and I will scrape her debris from her and

---

southern tribes, Judah and Benjamin, remained loyal to the crown and were led by Solomon's son, Rehoboam. The two kingdoms were at war during much of the subsequent two centuries.

make her a bare rock. She will be a place for the
spreading of nets . . . she will become spoil for the
nations. . . . I will bring upon Tyre from the north
Nebuchadnezzar king of Babylon, king of kings. . . . He
will slay your daughters on the mainland with the sword;
and he will make siege walls against you, cast up a
mound against you . . . battering rams he will direct
against your walls. . . . Also they will make spoil of your
riches . . . and throw your stones and your timbers and
your debris into the water. . . . You will be built no
more. (excerpts from Ezek. 26:2–14)

The proud city, which once boasted of possessing silver like dust
and gold like the mud in the streets (Zech. 9:3), withstood
Nebuchadnezzar's siege for nearly thirteen long years (585–573
B.C.). But in the end the king of Babylon triumphed, demolishing
the great walls and towers, leaving Tyre in ruins. The prophecy
had been partially fulfilled, but the *coup de grace* was not to come
until July 332 B.C.

THE END OF TYRE. Alexander the Great, whose mighty legions had
conquered the world, reached Tyre and demanded that the city
open its gates. Tyre refused. Alexander then devised a brilliant
strategy to take the city by force. He would build a causeway from
the mainland to the heavily fortified municipality.

The undertaking was immense. Alexander's army labored, taking
the stones, the timber, and the very dust of the city
Nebuchadnezzar had left in rubble and literally "threw the debris
into the water [sea]." By filling in the bay, an isthmus was formed
between the mainland and the city. Seven months later the
causeway was completed, and Alexander's troops marched across.
They defeated the Tyrian fleet, sacked the city, and burned it to
the ground. Every detail of God's verdict had been carried out
(Zech. 9:4), even to the forecast that Tyre would never be rebuilt
to its former glory.

However, the area of Tyre was still inhabited in our Lord's day.
On one of His visits there, He healed the daughter of a
Syrophoenician woman (Mark 7:24–30)—a rare case of conversion

to Christ recorded among the Phoenicians. Paul, too, stopped there for a week to fellowship in the Word with a group of believers (Acts 21:3–6).

Tyre was captured by the Muslims in A.D. 638. The city fell to the Crusaders in 1124, only to be recaptured and destroyed by the Muslims in 1291. Now a peninsula, Tyre is a town of no importance. A few thousand poor Persians and Arabs live in shabby hovels, and some Syrian fishermen "spread their nets." But the magnificence and fame of Tyre have vanished forever, gone the way of all nations who become anti-Semitic.

THE PHILISTINES

If ever there were a people whose name spelled trouble for the Jews, it was the Philistines. Their very existence and warlike nature, spiked by intense hatred of the Jews, constantly threatened the safety and survival of Israel. Who were these people, and from whence had they come?

The Philistines were non-Semitic, blond, blue-eyed Greeks. The descendants of Caphtor (Gen. 10:14), they are believed to have originated in Crete. They were a group of the sea peoples of the Mycenean civilization which was uprooted by the Dorians, another branch of Greeks. They had eventually settled in the southwestern region of the land God had deeded to the Jews. That conquered territory came to be known as Philistia—the land of the Philistines—and later as Palestine.

The Philistines worshiped the fish-god Dagon (1 Sam. 5:1–4), the fertility goddess Ashtaroth (1 Sam. 31:10), and Baal-zebub, chief god of Ekron (2 Kings 1:2ff). Like other Greeks, they occasionally offered human sacrifices, were generally degenerate, and frequently demon-possessed. They lived in opposition to *Yahweh*, the God of Israel.

Originally the governmental power of Philistia was vested in the lords of the Pentapolis (five city-states): Gaza, Ashkelon, Ashdod, Ekron, and Gath. The Philistines, hoping to dominate Israel, conducted frequent hit-and-run raids during the time of the Judges. Philistine victories were largely because of their superior weapons and their strict embargo against iron weapons for the Israelites (1 Sam. 13:19–22).

The Old Testament is replete with instances of Philistine antagonism toward the Jews. Nearly every child knows about Goliath, the gigantic challenger from Gath who dared defy the armies of the living God and met his death at the hand of a mere youth—David. Gaza, a disputed area in the present struggle of the Israelis and the Arabs, was the scene of Samson's famed exploits, humiliation, and victorious death. The Philistines contended for the very land God promised to Israel (Josh. 13:1–2), just as Palestinians do today.

In foretelling the fall of Tyre, Zechariah made reference to the subsequent judgment of Ashkelon, Gaza, Ekron, and Ashdod. Gath was not included for judgment having long since been captured by Hazael, king of Syria (2 Kings 12:17). The prophecy reads:

> Ashkelon will see it [the fall of Tyre] and be afraid [they surrendered]. Gaza too will writhe in great pain [Gaza resisted and was besieged by Alexander for five months]; also Ekron, for her expectation has been confounded [expected to be delivered but went into slavery instead]. Moreover, the king will perish from Gaza, and Ashkelon will not be inhabited [by the Philistines]. And a mongrel race [foreign people] will dwell in Ashdod, and I [God] will cut off the pride of the Philistines. And I will remove their blood [human sacrifices] from their mouth, and their detestable things from between their teeth. Then they also will be a remnant for our God [evangelism after disaster wins converts among the survivors], and be like a clan in Judah, and Ekron like a Jebusite [the original inhabitants of Jerusalem, then called Jebus]. (Zech. 9:5–7)

This prophecy too was fulfilled. The Philistines as a race were cut off. The only ones to outlive the destruction of their cities were those who believed in the promised Messiah and appreciated the Jews as the chosen nation from which Messiah would come.

4

Anti-Semitism in Modern History

RELIGIOUS PERSECUTION

ONE OF THE MOST UNENLIGHTENED PERIODS in Western European history was the Middle Ages, often referred to as the Dark Ages—the darkness of unbelief and superstition. Although the exact length of the Middle Ages is difficult to determine, the period generally encompasses the time between ancient and modern history. The era spans the time from the fall of the Western Roman Empire A.D. 476 to the beginning of the Reformation in the early sixteenth century. The duration was approximately one thousand years, during which the Jews of Europe struggled to survive.

Throughout the Middle Ages and up to the nineteenth century most of the opposition to the Jews came from organized religion. This opposition was based on the erroneous claim that the Jews were responsible for crucifying Christ and this had brought 'well-deserved' scorn upon themselves.[35]

---

35. Many zealous anti-Semites erroneously interpreted Matthew 27:25 as proof that the Jews asked for all the trouble and persecution which they received.

Fostered by constant agitation, anti-Semitism erupted sporadically and was expressed in terrible waves of abuse. Often the persecution imposed severe personal and economic restraints: confinement to the limits of a ghetto, disbarment from the more popular professions, and relegation to highly unpopular trades, such as usury. Despite these limitations many Jews prospered only to incite further resentment among their neighbors.

At times, the Jews were expelled from their countries of residence, and their mass immigration to other places of refuge helped only to brand them as aliens and intruders. The wandering Jew found no rest (Deut. 28:65). Yet the persecution and isolation of the Jews led to concentrated efforts to preserve their spiritual heritage.

The merger of church and state had given Romanism the impetus needed to dominate the people of Western Europe. Based on a misguided religiosity, the liberty to worship God according to the dictates of individual volition and the principles of doctrine set forth in Scripture were severely repressed. As early as 1215, this organized religion ruled that all Jews must wear circular badges of identification on their clothing. Books held sacred by the Jews were burned in public, and laws were enacted which restricted the Jews from living in the "Christian" community.

There were utterly ridiculous and unfounded claims of blood libel—that is, the accusation that the Jews murdered Christian infants to obtain blood for the Passover ritual. What was the motivation for such monstrous lies? The Jews were used as scapegoats. By pinning the blame for social and economic ills of the time on an unpopular minority, discontent found an outlet. Why not divert the attention of the malcontents from real problems and issues to that unfathomable enigma, the Jew, who always seemed to rise above his circumstances?

An unfortunate axiom of human nature states: A lie that contains a few grains of truth and is voiced loud and often enough will be believed. The gullible public swallowed the lie of Jewish guile. Massacre followed massacre. The Church stood by unable to restrain the bloodletting. Papal bulls (official releases) issued to rescind the lies had no effect. The damage had been done. Once anti-Semitism was released upon Europe the floodtide could not be halted. And so, in the name of Christianity, the Jews were hounded, tormented, murdered. No wonder that the very name of Christ has become a stumbling block to many Jewish people.

THE MEDIEVAL INQUISITION

Much has been written about the dreaded Inquisition which, ostensibly, had been established to eradicate heresy. The word "inquisition" means inquiry—an inquiry to determine whether an accused person was truly a heretic. The Medieval Inquisition began across Europe in 1233. A "grace" period of one month duration was offered to all who wished to abjure heresy (real or alleged), and a penance was prescribed for those who returned to "the faith." For others who could not be persuaded by threats, instruments of torture were prepared and a forced confession of guilt was obtained.

Most cases brought to trial led to conviction. The disposition and punishment of the guilty were the prerogative of the civil rulers, and the usual sentence was imprisonment and confiscation of property. Many were accused and dispossessed. Soon a system of blackmail, graft, and simony—the purchase or sale of ecclesiastical office—victimized all who sought to avoid the trials. Terrible though it was, the Medieval Inquisition was only a prelude to the Spanish Inquisition.

THE SPANISH INQUISITION

PRELUDE TO TERROR. Perhaps the zeal of the Catholic monarchs, Ferdinand V and Isabella I, to make Spain a purely Catholic nation was an effort to erase every last vestige of Moslem domination. The Berber conquerors, called the Moors, had crossed the Strait of Gibraltar into Spain in 711 and had ruled for five hundred years. Not until 1212, in the Battle of *Las Navas de Tolosa*, did Spain deter the last serious Islamic threat to Christian dominance. The Berbers were defeated, and in an atmosphere of ever-mounting religious fanaticism the slow process of unifying the land through warfare, marriage, and inheritance commenced.

By the year 1469 the marriage of Ferdinand and Isabella would lead to the union of Aragon and Castille. Spain was on the verge of reaching the zenith of greatness. With the exception of Granada and Navarre, Spain was firmly in the hands of Spaniards.[36]

Granada remained under Moorish influence. This part of Moorish Spain had a reputation for excellent craftsmanship, thriving industries, flourishing agriculture and commerce. In the Moorish cities, Moslems, Jews, and Christians enjoyed the blessings of material prosperity. To the Castilian nobles whose country was poor, the temptation to possess this prize became too great. The reconquest of Granada became imperative.

Previous attempts were made to convert the sizable population of Jews and Moslems to Catholicism, but no force had been exerted. Even in newly conquered provinces, Jews and Moors were tolerated. The Jews, especially, had served the Spanish monarchs well, providing a prosperous commercial class and an educated elite for many administrative posts. Yet the royal couple had one consuming ambition—to see all Spain brought under Roman Catholicism.

TORQUEMADA. In a fanatical fervor to achieve religious and national unification, Ferdinand and Isabella instituted the Spanish Inquisition in the year 1478, no doubt at the instigation of Thomas de Torquemada, a Dominican priest. Official consent from Pope Sixtus IV came reluctantly in 1482. The hierarchy in Rome regarded disdainfully this usurpation of ecclesiastical prerogative and political power by the Spanish monarch.

By the next year in an effort to regain a measure of control Sixtus IV named Torquemada the first inquisitor general. A sincere and incorruptible zealot, he assumed the high office rejoicing in his opportunity to serve Christ by hounding heretics. His appointment did not, however, give him the power to rid Spain of Jewry. But in 1484 Torquemada decreed twenty-eight articles that extended the power of inquisitors. They now could attack not only heresy and

---

36. Aragon and Valencia had a twenty percent and thirty percent minority population of Moors, respectively. *Encyclopaedia Britannica*, 1970 ed., s.v. "Spain," 1092.

apostasy but also witchcraft, bigamy, blasphemy, and usury. This latter offense was an open warrant against Jews.

Torquemada's enthusiasm in rigorously enforcing the Inquisition is well-documented. The hunt for heretics proved to be a lucrative business, and soon the coffers of the king and the Spanish church swelled with the confiscated wealth of the victims. Although in the beginning the Inquisition affected only Christians and converts to Catholicism, Jews soon found themselves sucked into the maelstrom of hatred and suspicion. Many were horribly tortured, strangled, or incinerated.

The fury of the Inquisition burned with unrelenting frenzy. Systematically Christians who, through the enlightenment of the Scriptures, dared to challenge the dogma, authority, and tyranny of the organized church, were consigned to the flames of the *autos-da-fe* (acts of faith). After days or even weeks of the most excruciating tortures imaginable, the fires of the stake were but a merciful release from their tormentors, an ushering into glory. Still Torquemada's misdirected zeal was not satiated. The next most likely victims to feel his ruthless persecution were the baptized but unconverted Jews tagged with the insulting epithet of *Marranos*, "swine."

Once Spain had been a place of refuge for the Jews, many of whom could trace their membership in the Catholic church to the sixth century reign of King Recared I, a Visigothic king of Spain (586–601). They had become so thoroughly assimilated into the fabric of Spanish life that they considered themselves Spaniards. Through ingenuity and energetic drive they had accumulated substantial wealth, and through marriage and title they had risen to lofty positions. Their influence was felt even in the highest circles, much to the consternation of intolerant clerics and nobles who were obsessed with the idea of Spanish "purity." Although labeled as "legal" Christians, these Jews became suspect of insincerity of faith.

To his everlasting credit, Sixtus IV was dismayed at the excesses of Torquemada. At first his objections to the illegal procedures were ignored, and his rebukes went unheeded. But in 1492 when Torquemada requested the expulsion of all Jews from Spain, Sixtus IV refused.

Torquemada then hounded Ferdinand and Isabella to banish all unconverted Jews. Further, he wanted Spain to purge all its Jewish population. The royal couple hesitated. The Jews were respected in Spain and they remembered that a Jew, Abraham Senior, had arranged their marriage. But under the continuous clamor of Torquemada for the expulsion of the Jews, the royal couple weakened. Despite the persuasive counterpleas of Don Isaac Abravanel, a wealthy influential rabbi who was the finance minister to the Court of Spain, they submitted to anti-Semitic pressure.

Jewish historians record that Don Isaac Abravanel offered Ferdinand and Isabella vast sums to allow the Jews to remain in Spain. The king and queen were tempted, but as they were about to accept, Torquemada, raising a crucifix over his head, rushed into the room accusing the monarchs of selling out their Lord as Judas Iscariot had done to Jesus. The king and queen, terrified by this outburst, meekly surrendered to fear and signed the order. At a time when Spain needed all possible economic resources to sustain her European ascendancy and growing overseas empire, she was deprived of her most valuable human asset, the Jews. Spain's emerging dominance wilted into certain decline.

DISASTER FOR SPAIN. This fateful decision by the Spanish monarchs was made the same year, the same month in which Columbus was authorized to set sail on his voyage to discover new trade routes. Ironically, he discovered a new world that would be a future haven for all who desired freedom from the tyranny of church and state—America.

The modern exodus from Spain was led by Don Abravanel. When the Inquisition began, Spain's Jewish population numbered about a half million people. Approximately one hundred fifty thousand remained at that time. Some fifty thousand embraced Catholicism, while ten thousand others perished. The rest eventually found refuge in Turkey, North Africa, Egypt, southern France, Holland, and northern Italy where Sixtus welcomed them into the Papal States. Others settled in Africa, Asia, and South America, where they were among the first settlers of that continent. Don Abravanel located in Italy and entered the service of the king of Naples and, later, that of the Doge of Venice.

In the decision by Ferdinand and Isabella to expel the Jews, Spain lost an incalculable treasure of merchants, craftsmen, scholars, physicians, and scientists, while the nations that received them benefited economically and intellectually. The Jewish middle class had been the backbone of Spain, even as the Huguenots would become the backbone of Prussia during the Seven Years' War. No modern nation can survive the loss of its middle class, the stabilizing influence on its economy. Those who dispossessed the Jews and greedily stepped into their place lacked the necessary qualifications to perpetuate prosperity. The Spanish Empire began to crumble and was lost forever during the reign of Philip II. Anti-Semitism had again brought judgment.

In relating the history of Spain, the *Columbia Encyclopedia* gives cognizance to this fact:

> . . . The expulsion of the Jews deprived Spain of a large part of its most useful and active population. Many went to the Levant and to the Netherlands, where their skills, capital, and commercial connections benefited their hosts. . . . The Jewish legacy to Spain and Western Europe is immense. . . . and Jewish scholars such as Maimonides had a major share in the development of Christian scholasticism.[37]

The fires of the Inquisition spread throughout most of Europe, raged out of control, and devastated nominal Christians, true believers, and Jews alike. By 1569, Western Europe, once the center of world Jewry, was practically devoid of Jews; their numbers decimated, the remnant had been cruelly driven out and banished. But their influx elsewhere—by invitation of governments of wisdom and vision—brought not only a population shift but a shift in industry and commerce with resultant prosperity for these nations.

---

37. 1950 ed., s.v. "Spain," 1863.

THE RISE AND DECLINE OF THE BRITISH EMPIRE

With the Reformation, Romanism could no longer stem the tide of a new spiritual awakening. Out of the fires of persecution and martyrdom came a strengthened faith and conviction based on a renewed interest in the Scriptures that swept through Germany, Switzerland, Scandinavia, Holland, France, Scotland, and England. Suddenly, fortune began to turn in favor of the Jews. Their allegiance became a matter of great importance to the embattled Roman Catholics and rising Protestants. Each faction hoped that an endorsement from the Jews would sway the yet uncommitted into their camp.

Max Dimont cites excerpts from an article written by Martin Luther in defense of the Protestant position. The article, penned in 1523 and entitled "That Jesus Was Born a Jew" strongly advocates the principle of pro-Semitism. Luther said in part:

> For they [the Catholics] have dealt with the Jews as if they were dogs and not human beings. They have done nothing for them but curse them and seize their wealth. I would advise and beg everybody to deal kindly with the Jews and to instruct them in Scriptures; in such a case we could expect them to come over to us. . . . We must receive them kindly and allow them to compete with us in earning a livelihood . . . and if some remain obstinate, what of it? Not everyone is a good Christian.[38]

Only when the Jews spurned his offer did Luther turn against them, as he later turned against others who had disillusioned and betrayed him. By then he was ill, discouraged, bitter, and torn over the disunion of faiths in his own country. Yet the first break between church and state had been made.

---

38. Max I. Dimont, *Jews, God and History* (New York: Simon and Schuster, 1962), 231.

THE ENGLISH CIVIL WAR

England's strong ties to Rome were severed during the reign of the Tudors. Then, the first civil war (the Puritan Revolution) brought a man of military genius to prominence and leadership. With Oliver Cromwell's defeat of the Cavaliers, those loyal to Charles I, feudalism ended in England and gave way to the incentive of capitalism.

As Lord Protector of England, Cromwell opened the door of divine blessing when he declared his country a haven for the Jews in 1655. He offered them citizenship and equal privileges with the English people. As a result the sun began to rise on the horizon of Britain and reached its apogee in the reign of Queen Victoria, when the sun literally never set on the Union Jack.

VICTORIAN ENGLAND

Several factors combined to make Great Britain a majestic empire. First of all, Queen Victoria was a believer, as was Albert, her consort. He is said to have found his strength in the Bible and in prayer, and his influence on Victoria's thinking was profound. Albert was a man of strong moral principles, irreproachable character, and high ideals. Thus, his keen and benevolent concern over the welfare of all British subjects marked the entire Victorian era as one of law and order and intense patriotism. Victoria's long and glorious reign was characterized by aggressive imperialism abroad and democratic principles at home.

Two of the most influential assets to Victoria's regime were Disraeli and Gladstone, both serving alternately as prime ministers in the later years. Never as popular with the Queen as Disraeli, Gladstone—himself a believer—is best known for his superior domestic politics.

On the other hand, Benjamin Disraeli, the first Earl of Beaconsfield, was a brilliant statesman in every respect. The son of Isaac D'Israeli, a Jewish convert to Christianity, he quite possibly was also a believer. Certainly he was the first Jew in modern history to have attained such renown in a great nation. Disraeli instituted improved domestic programs in housing, health, and working conditions—without socialism. Yet his fame rests on his ingenious foreign policy.

Through Disraeli's administration Britain consolidated and expanded as an imperial power. In 1876 Disraeli was instrumental in crowning Victoria Empress of India—the jewel in her crown. His purchase of the controlling shares in the Suez Canal gave Britain a powerful naval presence in the Mediterranean and access to India and the western Pacific. During his tenure of office, the Fiji Islands were annexed, Cyprus was ceded to Great Britain, and Russia's power was greatly reduced in the Balkans.

Two other Jews held positions of importance under Victoria: Sir Moses Montefiore, the Queen's financial adviser and founder of the Provisional Bank of Ireland, and Sir Rufus Isaacs, the first Jewish Chief Justice of England. Isaacs was subsequently knighted to serve as Viceroy of India.

An additional factor that served to bless Britain was the tremendous number of missionaries sent out to proclaim the Gospel of salvation to the uttermost parts of the empire. Yet Britain never used her power to coerce human volition where Christianity was concerned. Thus, Britain became a client nation to God in the last century:[39] She extended the Gospel of Jesus Christ, displayed a strong desire for the doctrines of God's Word, promoted a pro-Semitic attitude, and maintained the principles of the laws of divine establishment.[40]

BRITAIN AND ZIONISM

Toward the turn of the nineteenth century the Jewish dream of reestablishing a Jewish state gathered impetus and shape. Since their dispersion, A.D. 70, the Jews had clung tenaciously to the

---

39. A client nation is God's specifically protected representative on earth. The purpose of a client nation is to be the center of Bible teaching, evangelism, and missionary activity. See *The Divine Outline of History*, 35–37, 67–69.

40. These are principles set up by God for the survival, protection, perpetuation, and orderly function of the human race during the angelic conflict. See *Divine Establishment* (1988), 4–5, 90–93.

hope of being restored to Palestine. The continued persecutions they had suffered only strengthened the depth of yearning for the *aliyah*, the Hebrew word for the ascent or immigration to Palestine.

Orthodox Jews were still convinced that only Messiah should regather them. This, of course, is the biblically correct view of Israel's restoration to the Land. But so intense was this longing, born of suffering, that many Jews were ready even to follow self-styled, false Messiahs—Jewish mystics—into ventures which were doomed before they started. Eventually Jewish thinking changed. Since no Messianic regathering was forthcoming, as many came to believe, the people themselves would have to organize and, if need be, fight for their land. Zionism was born, and Jewish colonization of the Land began in 1870.

Zionism is strictly man's effort to usher in the Jewish Millennium.[41] As a religious and political movement its aims are to establish a Jewish homeland into which all Jews who wish might be admitted. From the Jewish point of view such a desire is understandable, and the vision, energy, and courage of the people who made the State of Israel a reality are truly admirable. The Bible neither condemns, condones, nor encourages any such effort. However, the Scriptures clearly indicate that during the Tribulation, unregenerate Israel will be regathered as a nation (Zech. 12—14) in its own right and in a position to draw and sign legitimate treaties.[42]

Early in the twentieth century the Jews sought to reclaim their land by purchasing large portions of arid and worthless real estate in Palestine. They paid the unreasonably high prices the Arab and Turkish landowners demanded and were only too happy to accept. Later, when thousands of Eastern European Jewish immigrants began to arrive, the Arabs began to consider themselves "dispossessed" and outnumbered by the Jews.

---

41. The term designates the promised kingdom of Messiah (Davidic Covenant) in which Messiah would defeat the armies of the world for Israel and reign for a thousand years (Rev. 19:19—20:4), restore Israel to the Promised Land, and make universal peace a reality on earth (Isa. 11; 35; 65:17—25).

42. If the Rapture of the Church were to occur in the very near future, then the current nation of Israel could be the nucleus of the regathering.

THE ADVANCE OF ZIONISM IN WORLD WAR I. During World War I, Turkey sided with the Central Powers (Germany and Austria-Hungary) against the British Empire. Turkey became a threat to both British and Zionist interests in the Middle East. Concurrently, the British war effort was being severely hampered for lack of acetone, a chemical which Great Britain had imported from Germany before the war. The chemical was essential to the manufacture of explosives.

In 1915, Dr. Chaim Weizmann (1874–1952) received a call to the British War Office. Weizmann was a brilliant Russian-born Jew and scientist, who had become an English subject in 1910 and was at this time the director of the British Admiralty Laboratories. He was presented with the problem: Could he produce a substitute for the acetone Britain so desperately needed? Weizmann promptly developed a perfect alternate substance—a synthetic cordite. He became a national hero overnight.

With Weizmann's charming personality, his indispensability to the war effort, and his contact with many important figures in England, he was able to exert considerable influence on a grateful British government. Prominent in the Zionist movement he was successful in obtaining the Balfour Declaration favoring the establishment of a Jewish homeland in Palestine. There was one condition: The rights of the non-Jewish communities in Palestine must be respected.

On paper the Balfour Declaration of 1917 was a triumph for the Jews. The British government would assume the protection of the Jews. In reality, however, things were not quite so simple. The fact that a Jew had turned the tide of battle in favor of the British and that Britain now championed the Jewish cause enraged the Turks and the Arabs. Any Jew in their territories who was suspected of the least pro-British sympathies was summarily hanged. Zionism was outlawed, and more than twelve thousand Jews were deported from Turkey.

ZIONISM BETWEEN THE WARS. In the peace conferences that followed the allied victory in World War I, the Middle East was neatly carved up into a series of small nations: Syria, Trans-Jordan, Saudi Arabia, and Lebanon. At the same time, the need for oil in Britain and France was becoming so vital that all treaties with these newly born Middle Eastern nations were designed to bind them to the allies. This is the genesis of Europe's dependence on Middle Eastern oil and their plight in the present crisis.

In 1923 Britain acquired a mandate over Palestine, which they enforced in accordance with the Balfour Declaration. During the first few years of the mandate, Jewish colonization of Palestine expanded rapidly but so did anti-Jewish sentiment on the part of the Arabs. By 1928, hatred between the Arabs and the Jews erupted in a clash over the Wailing Wall in Jerusalem. A major Arab revolt followed in 1929.

Britain was caught in the middle. They wanted to maintain amicable relations with the Arabs and also enforce the Balfour Declaration. The British peace-keeping forces achieved some semblance of order, but the controversy continued. As a compromise that pleased neither side, Britain sought to limit the influx of Jews and their purchase of land in Palestine. For the first time in hundreds of years Britain had made a decision detrimental to the Jews. This coincided with the initial disintegration of the British Empire.

Still another factor in Britain's fateful decision must be noted. This incident is connected with World War I and the defeat of the Turks. The British victory over the Turks occurred in such a way that it obligated them to the Arabs.

The name of Lawrence of Arabia is linked with romantic adventure, and the man himself became a legend in his own day. In reality, the famed British adventurer was a soldier and scholar who, in 1910, set out alone to walk across Syria. From Syria he joined archeological expeditions into the region of Arabia. During World War I, he was attached to British army intelligence and was instrumental in coordinating the Arab rebellion against the Turks.

In exchange for revolting against the Turks the Arabs were secretly promised certain Middle Eastern territories. Sir Arthur McMahon, Britain's Commissioner to Egypt, had put these promises in writing. Vaguely worded, Palestine was not mentioned in any of the communications. But to the Arabs the possession of that land was a foregone conclusion. Nor would they be reconciled to a Jewish presence in Palestine.

However, after World War I the flow of Jewish immigration to Palestine continued and by 1933 when Hitler rose to power, the flow became a flood. Alarmed that Palestine would be transformed into a Jewish state, the Arabs demanded that Britain put a stop to all Jewish immigration. One would have thought that the plight of the European Jews would arouse world opinion in favor of a Jewish exodus. Far from it!

Britain was in a quandary. They owed a debt to the Jews; they owed a debt to the Arabs. In 1936, Britain proposed to partition Palestine between the Jews and the Arabs, with a neutral sector between them. The Arabs again revolted. They claimed the right of national self-determination because Arabs represented the majority of the populace. The British repressed the revolt, often brutally, but actually sympathized with Arab nationalism and hegemony.

ZIONISM DURING AND AFTER WORLD WAR II. Before the outbreak of World War II, the British released a public document, the White Paper of 1939, which guaranteed the further decline of the Empire. The Paper announced British intentions to create in Palestine a predominantly Arab state. Jewish immigration was to be limited to only fifteen hundred persons per month and was to stop entirely by 1944 when the Jewish population of Palestine was expected to number five hundred thousand.[43]

Palestinian and world Jewry were outraged; but with the eruption of World War II, all differences were temporarily set aside. Political tension diminished. Because of its strategically important location, Palestine became an armed camp, a military defense base, with all parties aiding the British war effort in hopes of future favors.

In the years between the wars Dr. Weizmann was an honorary adviser to the British Ministry of Supply. He greatly advanced the research of synthetic rubber and high-octane gasoline, while continuing his campaign on behalf of Jewish immigration. The Jews already in Palestine also recognized that the doors must be kept

---

43. By comparison, in 1939 the combined Moslem and Christian population—mostly Arabs—numbered approximately one million people.

open for those who fled in ever increasing numbers from the horrors of Nazi persecution. Fewer and fewer countries were allowing European Jews to relocate within their borders.

During World War II one hundred thirty thousand Jews volunteered to enlist in the British Africa Corps, eager to meet the Nazis in combat. Yet only thirty thousand were accepted (not to exceed the number of Arab volunteers). Serving as independent companies, the Jewish Legion distinguished itself for valor in the North African campaigns and in Italy. How grateful would Great Britain be for Jewish contribution toward victory?

With the end of the war the terrible truth of the horrors of the Nazi concentration camps and Hitler's systematic extermination of six million Jews was exposed. The world was shocked. Hastily, refugee camps were set up for the piteous survivors of Nazi atrocities. Still Britain was intent on enforcing the policy specified in the White Paper. The Arabs were as implacable as ever and firmly opposed to any Jewish immigration.

With a determination born of frustration, desperation, and a will to survive, the Jews of Palestine came to the aid of their less fortunate brothers. They organized into tight-knit, combat-ready fighting units. Other Jews throughout the world financed the struggle. The Palestinian Jews smuggled in refugees right under the noses of the British in open defiance of their immigration quotas. The British intercepted the illegal immigrants and detained them on Cyprus. Mass arrests were made. Jewish leaders were captured and hanged. Yet the secret convoys kept coming, and Jewish determination to find a permanent solution to their dilemma was deepened by every act of reprisal.

In Parliament at that time, cautious and conciliatory voices were raised to reconsider Britain's attitude toward the Jews. But, handicapped by their allegiance to the Arabs, British leaders were deaf to those voices. The British military now became the most formidable enemy against Palestinian Jewish soldiers. This action would become a tragic mistake for the empire as the Union Jack was lowered over Palestine for the last time on 14 May 1948.

To Britain's credit, although the decision was anti-Jewish, British soldiers did not despise the Jews for their fervor. In fact, they had nothing but admiration for Jewish courage. Nor did the army lose because British troops were inferior to the Jewish combat teams. Britain lost the struggle in Palestine because of problems of greater precedence in other lands of her far-flung empire, which had begun to crumble. From the biblical view, however, Britain's loss in Palestine and decline elsewhere can be attributed to one fact only—anti-Semitism, the never-failing principle stated in Genesis 12:3.

Out of the Israeli War for Independence came the creation of the present Jewish State. Suffice it to say, Britain has paid dearly for her mistakes. Today, what remains of the British Empire—the United Kingdom—is beset with economic and political problems, plagued with terrorist attacks and bombings. Her glory lives on in history books and in the imagination of those who remember the "thin red line" that defended British sovereignty in every part of the world.

THE DREYFUS AFFAIR IN FRANCE

Not only do world empires collapse under anti-Semitic policies but the ruin of individual lives eventuates from this racial antagonism. In the process great personal injustice is inflicted on people simply because they are Jewish. A case in point was the *cause celebre* in France that became known around the world as the "Dreyfus Affair." This sordid business was entirely concocted by men of evil aspirations, intent on falsely accusing one Jew of espionage. Their purpose was to stereotype all Jews as potential subversives and declare them unfit for the officer corps of the French Army.

Alfred Dreyfus (1859–1935) was the son of a Jewish manufacturer who had immigrated to France after the cession of Alsace to Germany. Desiring to make the military his career, young Dreyfus became an artillery captain and was the first Jew in France to be appointed to a staff post. The appointment occasioned consternation and caustic objections, for the French army was permeated with anti-Semitism.

Dreyfus would have remained an obscure figure apart from the trumped-up charges in the case that bore his name. His contemporaries described him as a quiet, unassuming man with few friends. He was wealthy, happily married with two children. Thoroughly assimilated into the French upper class, he was known to have been a fervent patriot. Out of love of country he embarked on a military career.

But while all prosperous Jews were welcome in the elegant salons of society, the army denied loyal Jewish sons equal status with that of other Frenchmen. Political tradition ruled out Jewish career officers, and Roman Catholicism could not accept those who, by virtue of their beliefs, were beyond the influence of the confessional. Prejudice and animosity toward the Jews clearly set the stage on which this drama unfolded.

The scandal broke in 1894 when evidence surfaced that French military secrets had been betrayed to the Germans. Who was the turncoat in their midst? Calls to investigate were immediate. The evidence was slim—only a handwritten letter known as the *bordereau*, listing secret French documents, which the traitor had promised to deliver to Major Max von Schwartzkoppen, the German military attache in Paris. The only link between Dreyfus and the *bordereau* was the resemblance of the letter's text to his handwriting. There was no other proof of the captain's guilt.

That same year Dreyfus was arrested and charged with treason. In vain he protested his innocence. A court-martial convened under the influence of anti-Semitic officers. Captain Dreyfus was convicted, then sentenced to public degradation and life imprisonment on Devil's Island, Guiana.

The case might well have been forgotten were it not for the efforts of Lieutenant Colonel Georges Picquart, chief of the counter-intelligence section of the French Secret Service. Colonel Picquart came forth with new evidence in 1896 that cleared Dreyfus. The facts he had discovered placed guilt on a dashing aristocrat of Hungarian descent, Major Ferdinand Walsin Esterhazy, the true author of the forged *bordereau*. In order to pay outstanding debts, Esterhazy had resorted to the sale of military secrets to the Germans.

To the French General Staff, the indictment of an officer of nobility was unthinkable. A conviction would discredit the entire officer corps and undermine the public's confidence in the army.

Because the General Staff did not want to reopen the case, Colonel Picquart was ordered not to divulge his discovery. But Picquart's personal sense of justice was so strong that he persisted in his attempts on Dreyfus' behalf. Consequently, he was demoted and transferred to Tunis in the hope that he would be silenced. He was not! He was subsequently dismissed from the service, arrested, and charged with forgery in 1898.

Yet Picquart's fearless public statements aroused others. Working independently, Dreyfus' brother, Mathieu, exposed the same facts and pressed for a reopening of the case. Rapidly the Dreyfus affair became a major political issue. National tension mounted and for the next ten years the country was split into two factions—Dreyfusards and anti-Dreyfusards.

Concurrent with Colonel Picquart's forgery arrest, other deceptions began to surface. Major Hubert Joseph Henry, the original discoverer of the *bordereau*, had falsified new documents in an attempt to exonerate Esterhazy. From the beginning Major Henry had been one of the most vociferous antagonists of Dreyfus. In an effort to extricate the army from this tangled web of intrigue, Major Esterhazy was tried in a military court. The trial was another farce. Esterhazy was acquitted despite overwhelming evidence of his guilt, while Dreyfus continued to languish on Devil's Island.

In that same year renowned and passionate defenders of Dreyfus rallied to his cause, including Georges Clemenceau, who later become the Premier of France, Anatole France, and Emile Zola, the famous novelist and journalist. In his brilliant article "*J'accuse*" ("I accuse"), Zola exposed not a Jewish conspiracy against France but a conspiracy on the part of the military high command against the Jew, Dreyfus. This he termed to be a crime of "high treason against humanity." Zola, subsequently prosecuted and convicted for libel, fled to England to avoid prison.

Also in 1898 Joseph Henry, who had manufactured the evidence that sent Dreyfus to prison, committed suicide to shield his friend Esterhazy. Fully cognizant of these developments, the public clamored for a retrial of Dreyfus. Still, the anti-Semitic forces at work behind the scenes were so powerful that, despite the suicide and the presentation of new evidence, the military court at Rennes found Dreyfus guilty of "treason in extenuating circumstances." His sentence was reduced to ten years and finally he was pardoned for a crime he never committed.

By this time the Dreyfus affair had received worldwide notoriety. The uproar for the complete exoneration of Dreyfus continued unabated. In time Major Esterhazy was convicted of embezzlement and given a dishonorable discharge. He fled to England where, later, he admitted his complicity in the forgeries.

Meanwhile, France had elected a new premier—Georges Clemenceau. Under Clemenceau, Dreyfus was acquitted in 1906, reinstated in the army with the rank of major, and decorated with the Legion of Honor. The vindication of Dreyfus was simultaneous with that of Picquart, who rose to the rank of general and entered Clemenceau's cabinet as war minister. When World War I erupted, Dreyfus, too, was elevated to general. His innocence was proven beyond a shadow of a doubt in a publication of Schwartzkoppen's papers in 1930. Five years later, Dreyfus died. Yet his name lives on, linked with the grotesque miscarriage of justice that will remain forever a stain on the honor of France.

The courage of a fine soldier, Georges Picquart, and the great journalist, Emile Zola, helped to right this grievous wrong. In June of 1908, when the ashes of Zola were transferred to the Pantheon, Dreyfus was among those present to pay his personal respects to this man, who had refused to be blinded to the real issues of freedom and justice by the hysteria of anti-Semitism.

THE RISE AND FALL OF THE THIRD REICH

The most recent illustration of the tragic consequences accompanying anti-Semitism can be found in the downfall of the once proud German nation. The German descent into chaos can be attributed to one man, Adolph Hitler (1889–1945) and his Nazi ideology, woven into a central creed of anti-Semitism.

The infamy of Hitler's genocide against Christians and Jews bears the signs of possible demon possession. What else could explain his sudden advance from vagrancy to world prominence and power? What could induce the acclaim and adoration he exacted from his followers; the appalling violence he committed in his lust to exterminate all Jews; his wild hypnotic oratory and diatribes; his later drug addiction degenerating into ranting and raving until spittle covered his chin and jacket; and in the end, cowering in his bunker vindictively demanding Germany's total destruction as World War II drew to a close?[44]

HITLER'S BEGINNINGS

Consider this man's background. His father, Alois, was the illegitimate child of a peasant girl, Maria Anna Schicklgruber, and Johann Georg Heidler or Hitler. Though Alois was later legitimized, by German standards Adolph Hitler's social position scarcely recommended him for the leadership of that nation in the first half of the twentieth century. Adolph was born near the Bavarian border in the Austrian town of Braunau and from an early age he had but one aspiration—to become an artist.

After taking several preliminary art courses in Munich, he applied to the Vienna Academy of Art. His application was refused for his lack of talent. Frustrated by rejection, the poverty-stricken Hitler began nurturing a grudge against society. He became a brooding, solitary figure. He subsisted on a tiny inheritance and on the sale of several of his watercolors, which were of little artistic value.

In Vienna Hitler was first exposed to the venom of anti-Semitism. He came under the influence of Vienna's anti-Semitic mayor, Karl Lueger. This poison found fertile ground in his demented soul.

---

44. Demon possession is invasion and control of the body of an unbeliever by a fallen angel(s) (Dan. 10:20; Mark 5:1–13; Luke 4:32–36; 8:27; 9:39–40, 42; John 10:21). Certain characteristics of Hitler's abnormal behavior coincide with descriptions of demon possessed people in the Bible. The characteristics include convulsions (Mark 1:26; 9:20), violence (Matt. 8:28), raving (Mark 5:5), and foaming at the mouth (Mark 9:20; Luke 9:39). Possession can occur through idolatry, drug addiction, the phallic cult or other cultic religious activity, extreme or prolonged hatred or vengefulness, astrology and necromancy. Hitler was involved in most of these activities. See *Demonism*, 18–40, 62–64, 92–93.

When World War I broke out in 1914, Hitler enlisted in the army. He rose to the rank of corporal and was awarded the Iron Cross, first class, for bravery in Flanders. Yet he was not an outstanding soldier by any means. Later in the war, in a combat situation, he was exposed to poison gas and spent many months recovering in hospital. Possibly, at this point Satan chose to begin the infiltration of Hitler's mind with delusions of grandeur, for when the war was over, he moved back to Munich, determined to embark on a political career.

In Munich, Hitler joined a small band of malcontents and nationalist veterans who were rankled and bitter over Germany's capitulation and the severity of the Treaty of Versailles that ended World War I. By 1920, backed by a handful of faithful followers, Hitler emerged as the driving force behind the Nazi (National Socialist German Worker's) party. Slow to start, the party was destined to grow into a nightmare.

At first no one gave consideration to this megalomaniac whose life thus far had been a failure and whose abilities were less than mediocre. Only a few ex-army officers, among them Field Marshal von Ludendorff, believed that Hitler's personal magnetism could be harnessed for the rebuilding of the German military and German prestige. But Hitler had his own plans for power.

HITLER'S RISE TO POWER

The Treaty of Versailles had assigned the number of Germany's men under arms at one hundred thousand. But soon after their defeat German military minds devised an ingenious scheme to elude this treaty provision. This contrivance would build the finest military machine the world had ever seen. Every officer worth his mettle in the late war would be retained to hold a reserve commission. These men would serve in the guise of non-commissioned officers to train the *Wehrmacht* (German army). At the same time they would plan the future campaigns of the next war. Hitler and his fledgling party vigorously supported this military stratagem.

Ludendorff threw in his lot with Hitler, and together they organized an armed militia—the brown-shirted, jack-booted, swastika-armbanded storm troopers. Using this group of paramilitary thugs, Hitler hoped to bring all of Germany under his control. During 1923 in Munich, he attempted a *coup d'etat* which failed. Fourteen of the three thousand storm troopers, who had participated in the uprising, lay dead; many more were wounded, including one of Hitler's closest henchman, Hermann Goering.

The ringleaders, Ludendorff and Hitler, who had tried to flee, were arrested and the storm troopers banned. The prominence Ludendorff still enjoyed brought his immediate release, but Hitler was sentenced to a five-year term of which he served only thirteen months. During his imprisonment he wrote the manifesto that was to become the Nazi bible—*Mein Kampf* (*My Struggle*).

Temporarily, Germany breathed easier and forgot about Hitler. But the power-mad painter, who did not even possess German citizenship, had not forgotten his ambitious goal. When he left prison the nation was in social and economic chaos. The democratic but weak Weimar government was incapable of solving the mounting problems.

Meanwhile, the communists were gaining strength. Germany's elite—the militarists, monarchists, industrialists, and financial tycoons—feared the communists more than they feared the Socialists. They would turn to anyone who could defeat this menace. Ludendorff's association with Hitler had drawn their attention to the Nazis, and what Hitler propounded when he reentered politics made good sense to them. In Hitler's opinion, the blame for Germany's problems could be laid squarely at the doors of (1) the Treaty of Versailles, (2) the "Red Front" (communism), and (3) the Jews. He had a simple solution: Eliminate all three and restore Germany to its former greatness. This he proposed to do once he was in power. Victory and glory were certain.

To the amazement of outside observers, Hitler's party gained stronger representation in the *Reichstag* (the German Parliament) with each election. Although the aging General Paul von Hindenburg had been chosen president, he was a mere figurehead and scarcely in full possession of his faculties. Certainly he was no match for the wily Hitler. Unable to cope with the country's internal turmoil—those daily street fights between communists and Nazis—and faced with the threatened overthrow of the government, Hindenburg appointed Hitler Chancellor of Germany in 1933.

CONSOLIDATING HIS POWER. The appointment was the measure of legitimacy that Hitler needed to usurp all political authority for himself. So sure was he of his popularity that he dissolved the Reichstag and set a date for new elections on 5 March 1933. But the week before the voting, an arsonist torched the Reichstag building. Hitler who had personally ordered the burning blamed the communists for the incident. The public outrage at the communists was the pretext for unleashing Nazi storm troopers on all of Hitler's political rivals and real or suspected enemies. Anyone who disagreed with or opposed Hitler was summarily executed or disappeared into newly constructed concentration camps.

In a remarkably short time Hitler consolidated his position by eliminating most of his opposition. Those who escaped arrest kept quiet. But straight-thinking Germans were obviously alarmed at the thought of Hitler at the helm. No longer did Germany consider his strutting boastfulness comical, nor his goose-stepping storm troopers a laughing matter. The ruthless, dreaded *geheime staats polizei* (Gestapo—the Secret Police) were ubiquitous. So called 'enemies of the state' were dragged from their homes to Gestapo cellars where they were interrogated, tortured, and shot. Fresh in the memory of the citizenry was the 1934 blood purge of the Nazi party, "The Night of the Long Knives," when many of Hitler's old cronies from the Munich days were murdered.

Two years and one reign of terror later, Hitler had established an absolute dictatorship. His schemes were grandiose: Germany would succeed the Holy Roman Empire and the Hohenzollern Empire as the Third Reich (the Third Empire). According to his predictions and promise, the Third Reich would last a thousand years. It endured only twelve—twelve years too long!

GERMAN LIFE UNDER HITLER

If we could use but one word to describe Hitler's regime, it
would be the word *ersatz*, a common word in every German
household during World War II. It means "substitute." Removing
something of value requires a replacement. Hitler did just that. In
place of the old black, white, and red flag of Germany, up went
the swastika on its red banner. Long-accepted greetings gave way
to an outstretched arm and the salute "Heil Hitler" (hail Hitler).
To refuse the salute was tantamount to treason and made a
person subject to immediate suspicion.

Biblical Christianity, too, became a thing of the past. In its place,
the old Germanic gods were reintroduced and neopagan doctrines
so well suited to Nazi ideology were propagated. Some saw Hitler
as God.[45] These substitutions were equivalent to idolatry, a
trademark of demonism (1 Cor. 10:19-21).

The shock of Nazi dehumanization of the Jews has over-
shadowed Hitler's momentous persecution of Christians. Not to be
overlooked, seven million Christians were put to death in Nazi
Germany between 1933 and 1945. When a nation is deprived of
the very persons who preserve its existence (Matt. 5:13), that
nation faces certain disaster. Freedom of thought, so highly
treasured by German minds, was stifled by intimidation, and the
few voices raised in protest were quickly silenced.

Still a few courageous and dedicated men like Pastor Martin
Niemoeller remained outspoken critics of the Hitler regime.
Niemoeller publicly deplored Nazi interference with the function of
the German churches and denounced the rise of neopaganism. His
fearless stand for Christian principle and doctrine led to his arrest
in 1937 and his imprisonment from 1938 until 1945, when he was
liberated by the victorious Allies.

Hitler kept his promise to those who had propelled him to
power through an act of "legal revolution." (The outlawing of the
Communist party had given him the full majority he needed to

---

45. John Toland, *Adolph Hitler* (Garden City, New York: Doubleday & Company,
Inc., 1976), 359.

gain office.) Boosting German nationalism, he ordered the complete rearming of Germany, thus repudiating the Treaty of Versailles.

Like a snake Hitler's twisted plan began to uncoil. In 1938 he incorporated into the Fatherland several million German-speaking people by annexing Austria and forcing Czechoslovakia to cede the Sudetenland. His popularity soared. The nation could once more raise its head proudly and dream of conquering the world. The song, "Today We Own Germany; Tomorrow the Whole World," was on everyone's lips, even as the newly-propagated concept of the German "master race" took root in their hearts.

With Germans as the Aryan superrace, all other races were relegated to an inferior position. The sinister theories of racism were taught in all public schools. Full-blooded Aryans were pictured as tall, blond, and blue-eyed, and Jews as short, black-haired, dark-eyed, hook-nosed, and sallow-faced. Documenting proof of Aryan descent became an obsession with the Nazis, while Jewishness in itself became a crime. Hitler was now primed to turn his attention to the "final solution" of the Jewish problem.

The Jewish population of Germany was aghast at the developments as were clear thinking Gentiles. Except for isolated cases, German Jewry had enjoyed relative freedom from anti-Semitism. Now rampant prejudice loomed on their horizon.

Proverbs 22:3*a* says, "The prudent sees the evil and hides himself." All who could decipher the "handwriting on the wall" packed and left the country. The majority of the Jews, however, decided to adopt a wait-and-see attitude. They deluded themselves by wishful thinking, convinced that such things could not happen in a civilized country like Germany.

Hitler's appointment of the club-footed, undeniably brilliant Goebbels as Minister of Public "Enlightenment" (Propaganda Minister) did much to further the attainment of Hitler's evil goals. Totally loyal to the cause of National Socialism and to Hitler, Goebbels used every available means of communication in manipulating the German people. He issued a deluge of slogans; he published blatant lies and declared them to be emphatic truths; he elevated Hitler to the status of demigod and whipped the citizenry into a frenzied worship of *der Fuehrer.*

The people were mesmerized. The young flocked to the Hitler Youth organization to be steeped in the dogmas of Nazi ideology. The general populace appeared content to follow their leader blindly wherever he might lead them—right down the path of national suicide.

How far might Germany have gone were it not for anti-Semitism? By the outbreak of World War II, Germany could boast of having the most formidable military machine in the world. The Wehrmacht had brilliant leadership. The *Luftwaffe* (air force) was advanced far beyond its time. The German fleet staffed with naval experts was imposing, complete with surface ships and submarines. The German army was well-prepared and motivated, having but one objective—supremacy of the Fatherland. The people were industrious and patriotic, willing to sacrifice all for the establishment of the new superrace. Yet from the beginning the possibility of German greatness was overruled by their attitude toward the Jews.

HITLER'S JEWISH SOLUTION

Hitler's "solution" to the "Jewish problem" evolved in stages, each progressively more evil. In 1933, the Nazis had been content with the boycott and looting of Jewish shops. Occasionally stores were vandalized and Jewish owners beaten.

Two years later, the enactment of the Nuremberg Laws deprived Jews of their citizenship, their businesses, their most basic civil rights. The "Jew ban" went into effect. The law forbade Jews to engage in professions. They could no longer frequent theatres, museums, and other public places. Shopping was restricted to certain stores during certain hours.

Jews could only have Jewish names. Those who had been given Teutonic names at birth were required to add the names "Sarah" or "Israel."

Intermarriage between Jews and Aryans was outlawed, and Aryan partners of preexisting marriages were pressured to leave their spouses and families. Jewish children were expelled from public schools.

On 9 November 1938 the Nazis launched a systematic campaign of terror against German Jews. *Kristallnacht,* "the night of glass," so-called because of the shattered glass of Jewish shops and the looting of synagogues all over Germany, marked the most vicious form yet of Nazi anti-Semitism.

The Jews still remaining in Germany were advised that their entire wealth would be confiscated and turned over to the German state, should they desire to leave the country. At the same time, the Nazis contrived a plan to hold all German Jews as hostages pending the payment of a ransom of one-and-a-half billion Reichsmarks. Geneva, Switzerland, was to be the site of the negotiations for the ransom to be paid by world Jewry. However, after the occupation of Czechoslovakia and invasion of Poland, the Germans broke off negotiations.

By 1940, the deportation of all German and Austrian Jews to specially created ghettos in Poland was a *fait accompli.* There they were abandoned to disease and starvation. But the "final solution" was not instituted until 1941, after Hitler invaded Russia. The primary principle of Hitler's eastward expansion was to secure *lebensraum,* "living space," for pureblooded Germans. Other inferior races must be eliminated in order to give every true Aryan a piece of soil to call his own.

Concentration camps in the east, which had thus far been used only to detain the Jews, were now to become extermination camps. Hitler's "solution" included not only the mass murder of all European Jews but also the enslavement and eventual liquidation of that segment of Eastern Europeans whom Hitler called *untermenschen,* "Christian subhumans."

With that sadistic goal in view the Nazis began mass deportations of young and healthy "subhumans" who could be forced to work for the Reich war effort. The Nazis efficiently concluded that this slave labor would free Germans to fight at the front. They conducted this conspiracy of dehumanization like a business. Inmates were estimated to work on an average of two hundred and seventy days before they dropped dead. Within five years of the inception of Hitler's fiendish plan, nearly three-quarter million Russians, Poles, Yugoslavs, and even Belgians and Dutch were uprooted from their native lands and "exported" to Germany.

Slave labor camps became commonplace over the countryside of Germany and German-occupied territory. Here these captives of the Nazis were underfed and overworked by their German masters until they became weak and ill. Special task forces were created for the sole purpose of expediting the extermination of the now useless slave laborers. These brutal units were composed mostly of Nazi party members who had *volunteered* for that job.

In the eastern conquered territories the systematic elimination of the Jews and Christians came in the wake of the invading Wehrmacht. Special Action Groups—Hitler's executioners, each group under the command of a general of the army—followed the occupation forces rounding up all known Jewish and Christian undesirables. These "expendables" were marched to a deserted area and forced to dig large pits or trenches. With their graves ready, they were ordered to undress and line up to be mowed down by machine guns. The dead were bulldozed into the mass graves and the wounded among the corpses were buried alive.

But the slaughter was not swift enough to satisfy the Fuehrer. Germany and Europe had to be rendered *Judenrein*, "purified of Jews," in a more efficient, less costly, and less tedious way. How could the mass murder of the Jews be facilitated? History credits the ruthless and most inhumane of all Nazi henchmen, Heinrich Himmler, with the introduction of gas chambers.

The problem was resolved in what Himmler considered to be a "humane" way: through the utilization of Zyklon B, a hydrogen cyanide gas, which was simple and inexpensive to manufacture. The mammoth task was handed over to Adolf Eichman, a lieutenant colonel in the storm troopers. When Germany surrendered, Eichman fled to South America where, fifteen years later, Israeli agents finally apprehended him. He was extradited to Israel, tried, and hanged in 1962 as a war criminal.

Eichman enthusiastically implemented the task assigned to him. Additional extermination camps had to be built and the existing ones adapted or modernized for this calculated mass murder. The camps had to be staffed with continuously brainwashed personnel who regarded all Jews as vermin.

A system for transporting the doomed victims was put into operation: Railroad spurs that led off the main lines were laid to take the Jews to their tragic destination. The Jews often thought they had purchased a ticket to freedom. Those who survived the brutal journey in overcrowded boxcars jammed with humanity, with no food or water, discovered too late that their only release would be from this world.

Another quote from Max I. Dimont presents a horrifying account of the Nazis' use of technology in the final disposal of the Jews:

> Soon a sizable segment of the German population was diverted from the war effort for the planning, building, and staffing of these murder camps. Generals on the Russian front complained that winter uniforms for the troops were arriving late because trains had been diverted; industrialists complained they were being pirated of skilled labor. But nothing was allowed to interfere with the "final solution."
>
> Though there was a shortage of steel for tanks and airplanes, there was no shortage of steel to build furnaces for the disposal of the cadavers. This excerpt from a business letter from the Director of the Didier Works in Berlin gives proof of the knowledge German industrialists had of the use of their products:
>
> "For placing the bodies into the furnaces, we suggest simply a metal tray moving on cylinders. Each furnace will have an oven measuring only 24 by 18 inches, as coffins will not be used. For transporting corpses from the storage points to the furnaces we suggest using light carts on wheels, and we enclose diagrams of these drawn to scale."
>
> With German efficiency, chambers for the administration of Zyklon B gas were built to resemble large shower rooms. Arrivals were informed they would have to take a shower, were ordered to undress, and then herded into the "shower rooms." Small children were often thrown in after the adults. The steel doors to the gas chambers were shut. Then the amethyst-blue Zyklon B crystals were funneled through the large-holed

shower nozzles into the hermetically-sealed room. The hydrogen cyanide gas released from the crystals slowly rose to the ceiling, slowly gassing the people in the room, slowly turning the gasping, retching bodies into bright pink, green-spotted, convulsed corpses. Peepholes in walls and ceiling, protected by safety glass, were provided for Nazi officials who had a compulsion to view the agonized writhings of naked men and women choking to death. Through these peepholes they could watch, entranced, several performances a day.

New industries develop special skills, and the concentration camp industry was no exception. Adept *sonderkommandos* [specialized details] learned to apply grappling hooks with skill to separate the bodies. Trained technicians learned to pry dead lips apart and deftly knock out gold-filled teeth. Talented barbers dexterously shaved the heads of dead women. Six days a week, the new elite worked in the concentration camps. On Sunday they rested, went to church with their wives and children, and after church talked with horror about the eastern front, where Russians were killing German soldiers, and commented on the barbarity of the Americans who were dropping bombs on civilians.

At the Auschwitz concentration camp 7000 Germans were thus employed. Here seventeen tons of gold were collected from the teeth of the dead. The hair from the shaven heads were used in the manufacture of cloth and mattresses. The ashes of the bodies were used as fertilizer for German victory gardens. Fatty acids were salvaged for making inexpensive soap. This is a good formula, according to a Danzig firm: "Take 12 pounds of human fat, 10 quarts of water, and 8 ounces to a pound of caustic soda and boil for two or three hours, then cool."[46]

---

46. *Jews, God and History*, 381–82.

All these details, of course, were kept in strict secret until after the war, when the appalling truth was discovered. The Nuremberg trials revealed barbarous cruelty, sadistic medical experiments practiced on countless victims whose sole crime was their Jewishness. At the Auschwitz concentration camp alone four million Jews lost their lives in gas chambers, medical experimentation, or to shooting, hanging, beating, malnutrition, and disease.[47] These acts of brutality are documented but are too horrible to describe in graphic detail.

The question has often been asked why the Jews did not resist the Nazis. The answer is simple: Neither the Jews nor the outside world knew of Hitler's final solution to the Jewish problem. Reports of what was happening in the concentration camps were considered rumors; no one believed that such inhumanity could possibly exist in the twentieth century.

By 1943, however, there could be no further doubt that the terrible rumors that filtered out were all too true. By then it was too late; the Jews could not defend themselves. Their leadership had been murdered, their communities dispersed, and their numbers decimated. They had nothing with which to fight back— only their will to survive—and that will was phenomenally strong. The unbelievable tenacity of inmates of the concentration camps kept them from going insane or committing suicide.

In some instances, as in the Warsaw ghetto uprising in 1943, Jews did stage a valiant armed resistance. That ghetto had been used as a collection point for Jews designated to be shipped to death camps. Against overwhelming odds, the Jews held out for six weeks and even routed the Nazis. With what, you ask? With weapons, many of them outdated, that they had obtained through bribes, raids, and Jewish ingenuity.

A special combat group had to be summoned to deal with the uprising. Continued artillery barrages turned the ghetto into a blazing inferno. More artillery shells were required to subdue and

---

47. The *Encyclopaedia Judaica* devotes two hundred forty thousand words, contributed by 109 writers and editors on the subject of the "holocaust." All known facts and statistics are listed and many of the atrocities illustrated. The shocking horror of it all makes virulent reading.

defeat a few determined Jews in that one sector of Warsaw than to originally capture the entire city! For this act of "bravery," General Juergen Stroop was awarded an Iron Cross. After 1943 no large number of Jews were concentrated in any one sector outside the death camps.

The circumstances surrounding the defeat of the courageous Jews are significant, illustrating once again the principle of the curse of Genesis 12:3. When the hard-pressed defenders of the ghetto appealed urgently to the Polish underground to come to the rescue against their common German enemy, the Poles refused. They had no love for the Jews. However, with the Russian army at the gates of Warsaw in late 1944, the Polish underground at last attacked the Germans and, in turn, called on the Russians to assist them. The Russians refused. As a result the entire underground, numbering fifteen thousand men, was wiped out.

By 1943 the speed with which the Nazi executioners liquidated the remaining Jews was accelerated. Even after the tide of battle turned and the Nazis began to retreat, the death trains with their cargo of human misery continued to roll. The rapid Allied advance across Germany's frontier occasioned a frantic effort to obliterate any traces of the death camps. Too late! In Poland alone, enough Zyklon B crystals were found to gas twenty million more people, along with Nazi plans which called for the slaughter of ten million non-Germans every year after victory. The sites of these mass murders remain as monuments to Nazi atrocities.

On the other side of this ghastly picture, history has recorded countless acts of heroism on the part of individuals and entire populations who refused to surrender Jews living in their midst to Nazi tormentors. For their heroic stand many forfeited their lives. Among those gallant nations were France, Belgium, Holland, Yugoslavia, and even Hitler's ally Italy.

Outstanding for their efforts in the cause of pro-Semitism were the Danes and the Norwegians. Reportedly the king of Denmark personally took part in the organization of an underground, composed of a flotilla of fishing boats to assist Jews in their escape. More than that, he wore a yellow Star of David in public to show his sympathy for the plight of the Jews.

Finland threatened to declare war on Germany if any of her

Jewish citizens were harmed. Yugoslavia and Greece flatly refused to cooperate with the Germans if one Jew was touched by the Nazis. Not so Poland! Without a single voice raised in protest, Poland handed over its Jewish population for slaughter. They paid dearly for their anti-Semitism. While Finland has enjoyed at least some measure of independence, Poland would spend the next forty-five years under Soviet domination, from which it has not recovered.

Nazi anti-Semitism exacted a terrible toll. There were seventeen million battle casualties; eighteen million civilians perished as a direct result of warfare, and twelve million people were murdered by the Nazis. The truth about the death camps was no longer a guarded secret—it shook the world. The sight gagged battle-hardened American G.I.'s, who walked into concentration camps to liberate the dazed, half-starved, hollow-eyed survivors. They had lost all but their lives.

What did Nazi anti-Semitism cost the Germans? Max Dimont describes the price.

> The Germans who in 1933 had jubilantly 'heiled' their Fuehrer, could now mournfully count their dead: 3,250,000 battle deaths, 3,350,000 civilian dead, and some 5,000,000 wounded. Of 20,000,000 buildings, 7,000,000 were completely destroyed or severely damaged. The Germans, who time after time had complained to the world that they were destitute . . . somehow found $272,000,000,000 to spend for their six-year war. Hitlers do not come cheap.[48]

All the atrocities cannot be described in this brief space. Yet you should be aware that the United States of America was spared like cruelty by the bravery of our fighting men who have insured our freedom and secured our escape from a similar fate. This is one reason why I frequently honor the military from this pulpit. Their sacrifice has preserved our right and privilege to assemble and study the Word of God daily.

---

48. *Jews, God and History*, 387.

Thank God for those heroes, and pray for our men in uniform as you have never prayed before. Only our attitude of pro-Semitism and the deeds of our stalwart military have saved this country from the doom of Nazi Germany.

HITLER'S DEMON POSSESSION?

In Hitler, Satan found a willing and eager vehicle, considering this man's twisted soul, his thwarted ambitions, his grudge against society, his vicious hatred of Jews and Christians. His dabbling in astrology and neopaganism would afford easy access to satanic viewpoint and influence. He would readily seize the devil's offer: " . . . All these things will I give you . . . " (Matt. 4:9).

Apart from the explanation of demon possession, it would be improbable for a man of Hitler's mediocre abilities and lackluster personality to command the near worship or to formulate the sinister policies he instituted. The hypnotic magnetism he exuded could only be Satan-endued, as were the fiendish tactics that put Hitler's schemes into operation. This attempt to exterminate the Jews on a scale never before seen in history marks a desperate satanic maneuver. Satan realizes that the time for his opposition to the plan of God is rapidly running out.

Not until the Hitler era did racism really come into its own where the Jew was concerned. Prior religious, individual, and economic anti-Semitic prejudices were replaced by irrational racial bias and mass hysteria on a national scale. The fabric woven from the myth of a German superrace was manufactured out of the pit of hell, as were the atrocities this evil spawned.

On the one hand, the myth of racial superiority implanted in the German minds accentuated their place of power. Intoxicated with the illusion of their nation as supreme and the world groveling at their feet, they adored their beloved Fuehrer for perpetrating this pretentious goal. On the other hand, this man was more than power-mad; he was evil personified. His authority was established through terror, his followers held by fear dared not incur his rage.

Who were these people with whom Hitler surrounded himself, his elite inner circle? What were they like? Skilled statesmen?

Suave politicians? Polished diplomats? No! They were a motley array of sadists, masochists, murderers, drug addicts, and sex perverts.

Only a demon-possessed mind revels in such company that allows every evil and malignant impulse of the old sin nature free rein and expression. By removing all restraints from the old sin nature, by organizing and legalizing brutality—even rewarding the perpetrators with the confiscated wealth of Nazi victims—Hitler maintained his hellish followers. The fact that such men and women, the very dregs of humanity, were elevated to the highest offices demonstrates to what heights degenerates can ascend in Satan's domain.

Satan must have been exultant during those twelve years of murderous orgy. His kingdom was rid of millions of "undesirable aliens"—Jews and Christians. But Jesus Christ still controls history. Anti-Semitism cannot go unpunished indefinitely. God will never allow the complete destruction of the Jew. Although He may use such disaster for the discipline of a "stiff-necked people" and remind them of their need to turn to *Yahweh* (Lev. 26:14–46; Deut. 28), He continues to preserve His chosen people.

When the end did come, the "glorious" Third Reich went down ingloriously. The master race was overwhelmed by "inferiors." Those who had once hailed the Fuehrer now hailed the liberators with equal fervor. Once they had sworn undying loyalty to the Nazi regime; now they hastily discarded their uniforms and claimed they were unwilling dupes. As for their Fuehrer—they alleged to have never really supported him; they had always held that he was nothing but a madman, a murderer, an evil man.

And the Fuehrer? The Fuehrer lay dead in an underground bunker in blazing Berlin. On 30 April 1945, he shot himself through the mouth. His gasoline-drenched body was dumped in a shell crater outside the bunker and burned beyond recognition. His day of infamy was over; an era of ignominy had finally ended. Hitler was survived by the very Jews whom he had sworn to eradicate from the face of Europe.

In the days that followed World War II, all known Nazi collaborators were brought to justice. In the end, they, too, became the victims of the evil system they had served with such enthusiasm.

A principle of Scripture was thus fulfilled in the destruction of the destroyer.

> Behold, he travails [labors] with wickedness, and he conceives mischief [becomes pregnant with sin], and brings forth [gives birth to] falsehood [a life of deceit]. He has dug a pit and hollowed it out, and has fallen into the hole which he made. His mischief [sin, perverseness] will return upon his own head, and his violence will descend upon his own pate [top of his head]. (Ps. 7:14–16)

AMERICA AND ANTI-SEMITISM

The United States cannot afford anti-Semitism. There are too many examples of tragedies that befall nations which either turn their backs on the Jews or actively persecute them. This raises a serious question: How real is the existence and threat of anti-Semitism in the United States of America, a land traditionally known as a haven for all freedom-loving people?

As a nation, America has generally deplored anti-Semitism. In fact, our Constitution precludes it. Like all who have chosen to come to our shores, the Jews have been absorbed into the tapestry of freedoms unique to the American way of life. They are accorded the same privileges and status which the Constitution guarantees all law-abiding citizens, regardless of origin, race, or creed. They have equal opportunities and equal responsibilities.

Contrary to present popular ideas, there are no "hyphenated Americans." Either you are an American, or you are not. Too often today new immigrants and already established ethnic groups demand the retention and recognition of their old cultural standards which fragment rather than unify our society.

The history of the Jew in America has been one of mutual blessing. The Jews have personally benefited from the freedom and opportunity they enjoy here, and the United States, providing a refuge for them, has been richly blessed by God. Let us continue to hope and pray that Jews will always be welcome in this country.

Association with Jews began in 1621, when the first large scale Jewish immigration arrived from Spain. Yet Jews landed on American soil long before then. Records show Jews served in Columbus' small flotilla as able-bodied seamen, map readers, interpreters, and surgeons. In fact, efforts of Jewish scientists and cartographers, men like Abraham Cresques and his son Judah who first charted navigational maps, facilitated Spanish explorers in finding their way across the ocean.

A considerable number of prominent people in American history were Jews. Jews fought in the first War for Independence; Jewish financiers backed and honored the virtually worthless bills of exchange to procure supplies for the Continental Army of General Washington. Haym Solomon donated his entire personal fortune to the noble cause.

Jews have supported this country in all of her wars. They fought in the War of 1812 and in the Mexican War. Moses Albert Levy, a surgeon, and Abraham Wolf, a soldier, fought and died gallantly at the Alamo. Jews eagerly joined the ranks against Germany in the First and Second World Wars. Many of our finest officers and leaders were Jews.

The roster of outstanding American Jews is impressive. This illustrious group includes business and professional men, scientists and artists. Jewish financiers and philanthropists such as the Rosenwalds, the Guggenheims, and Nathan Straus have enriched our museums with their generous donations and fabulous art collections. They also established concert halls and theatres, as well as hospitals, schools, and homes for the aged.

Jews have enriched American lives by contributing to our musical and theatrical heritage. Who has not hummed the patriotic tune "God Bless America" or the holiday favorite "White Christmas" by Irving Berlin? Whose heart has not been stirred by the challenge of Sigmund Romberg's "Stouthearted Men"? The musicals of Jerome Kern and the classics of George and Ira Gershwin are as synonymous with American music as the sounds of Benny Goodman's orchestra are to the big band era. Many superb plays and books have come from the pen of a Jew, and America's motion picture industry owes its very existence to Jewish entrepreneurs like Louis B. Mayer and Samuel Goldwyn.

Brilliant Jewish minds like Jonas Salk furthered medicine by developing an effective vaccine against polio and isolating streptomycin. A Jew first discovered vitamins. Jews greatly advanced scientific farming in our nation. A. A. Michelson measured the velocity of light. Albert Einstein changed forever the world of physics by his experiments in the theory of relativity, statistical mechanics, and the photon theory of light. In short, Jews were prominent among those who helped make America the most advanced country on earth.

Their endeavors, combined with the industry of the new Jewish immigrants, ensured that their poor would not become a burden on the state. Characteristically, despite the squalor from which many of the penniless Jewish refugees began their climb up the ladder of success, families stayed intact. Crime, immorality, and illegitimacy were kept to a minimum. Defeatism and resignation to life in the slums were practically nonexistent.

Until the year 1880, anti-Semitism was virtually unknown in these United States. America needed people and welcomed all who would make their home here. Those who did come knew the value of freedom. They had experienced discrimination or persecution and had left the old country to make a life for themselves in the new world where people were accepted on their own merit. They could go as far as their inclination and ability would take them. The essence of Americanism is "that all men are . . . endowed by their Creator with certain inalienable Rights, that among these are Life, Liberty and the Pursuit of Happiness."[49]

Anti-Semitism is anti-American. This virulent curse found its way across the ocean from northern and eastern Europe, where it intensified toward the end of the nineteenth century. As European immigrants poured into this land of opportunity, they brought with them not only their skills and their culture but some brought their prejudices.

These bigots failed to see that America's greatness is built on free enterprise and contributions by all its citizens. They feared that the Jews would crowd them out of business and professions

---

49. The unanimous declaration of the Thirteen States.

as they had allegedly done in Europe. Clannishly, they stuck together in their own neighborhoods and social circles, excluding the Jews. They missed the invigorating experience that comes from mingling with new ideas and cultures.

Certainly, some enterprising Jews, who had started business with a peddler's tray on a street corner, rapidly expanded their investments into shops. Shops grew into department stores and accumulated fortunes for their owners. But the same was true of enterprising Gentiles. Far from being restrictive, competition in business stimulates growth and creates wealth which energizes the economy of a nation. What is detrimental to any society is deeply ingrained prejudice.

Prejudice is a preconceived opinion excluding reason or fair discernment of facts. Prejudice is a manifestation of jealousy and pettiness motivated by arrogance. Intolerant people are quick to believe hearsay, especially when it is damaging to others. And prejudice, whether carefully ingrained or superficially acquired, is difficult to overcome.

Prejudice concerning the Jew is suicidal to any nation. To America's credit, although there are currently signs of a marked increase in anti-Semitism, we have never permitted this blight to become rampant in our country.

Anti-Semitism surfaced briefly immediately preceding World War I and again in the 1930's. Before World War II, anti-Semitism was revived largely by instigation from Germany. With the revival in the 1940's, a new phenomenon emerged in American thinking; in a land which had long welcomed all foreigners, certain ethnic groups were singled out. Anti-Semites were emboldened by the increasing tendency to blame the Jews for national problems. Attempts to limit immigration primarily affected the Jews.[50] Rational Americans were deeply disturbed by those trends and tried to right this wrong.

---

50. The same situation is occurring today. In 1989 the United States set down new quotas for the immigration of Soviet citizens. At the moment when hundreds of thousands, mostly Jews, are free to leave Russia for the first time, no more than fifty thousand a year will find refuge in America. See Danielle Pletka, " Exodus A Godsend for Israel," *Insight* 6 (21 May 1990): 19; and "Soviet Jews Finding Themselves Stranded," *The Houston Post*, 3 March 1990, Editorial section, A-33.

The following is a quotation from Mrs. Theodore Roosevelt, Jr.:

> During the years immediately before World War II
> Ted [Roosevelt, Jr.] was troubled by the increase of
> anti-Semitism in the country. Believing that this could be
> fought more effectively by Christians than by the Jews
> themselves, he brought the subject up in every speech
> he made. In answer to a letter he received in 1941
> saying that it was the Jews themselves who were
> primarily responsible for this intolerance, he wrote:
>
> "From the standpoint of this country the question of
> who is responsible in whole or in part is entirely beside
> the point. The fact is that we hurt ourselves—the
> United States—more by persecuting the Jews than we
> hurt the Jews. If we persecute any racial or religious
> group we are committing a grave offense against our
> concept of government."[51]

ANTI-SEMITISM AND CONSERVATIVE POLITICS

Anti-Semitism expresses itself chiefly in three areas: socio-
economic, religious, and political. Regardless of where anti-
Semitism occurs, the destructive force is eventually identifiable.

A case in point concerns American conservatism. Conservatives
are primarily interested in the good of America, strongly adhere to
the principles of freedom and divine establishment, and are
intensely patriotic. But for decades they have had difficulty
establishing political influence. Liberalism has held sway in the
political, social, and philosophical arenas of the United States. One
reason: Unenlightened or misguided conservatives often take anti-
Semitic positions.

The conservative movement has been infiltrated by an anti-
Semitic element that castigates Jews as "generally liberal and left
wing." Consequently, enough conservatives have fallen prey to
anti-Semitic conspiracy theories that the overall movement has
been damaged. Regardless of how politically astute a conservative

---

51. *Day Before Yesterday* (Garden City, New York: Doubleday and Company,
1959), 417.

may be, if he becomes anti-Semitic he no longer represents America's best interest.

Anti-Semitism has blinded many to the true issues facing our nation. Misunderstanding the communist conspiracies, virulent anti-Semites have attributed the source of these conspiracies to the Jews. The fact that Marx and Trotsky—two of the progenitors of communist ideology—were born of Jewish parents in no wise implies the guilt of all Jews or justifies their condemnation. Engels, Marx's closest collaborator, was instrumental in developing communist philosophy, yet he had no Jewish family connection whatsoever.

Marx, baptized and brought up a Christian, later repudiated Christianity and Judaism. He was influenced by anti-Jewish ideas that were rampant in socialist circles of the last century. His famous essay "On the Jewish Question," published in 1844, was a classic of anti-Semitic propaganda. In this, Marx identified the Jew with all the most disagreeable characteristics of the greedy and predatory capitalist order which he was seeking to overthrow.[52] Of course, Marxist socialism of the type adopted by the Soviet Union and her satellites has been a miserable failure.

Trotsky was a nonprofessing Jew, an intellectual idealist and revolutionary, whose long feud with Stalin incurred Soviet discrimination against the Jews of Soviet Russia. None of these men are representative of the Jewish people. If anything, Russia's treatment of its Jewish population should convince misguided conservatives that communism and Judaism are antithetical.

THE SOLUTION TO ANTI-SEMITIC PREJUDICE

The irrational belief in Jewish conspiracy theories has translated into genuine hostility. The Jews have become the perfect "whipping boys" for all manner of financial, political, and social calamities surrounding humanity. Whatever your political persuasion, you should not distort the truth and insist that the Jew is the root of all the world's problems. Never propose that any problem would be solved by being rid of the Jew.

---

52. Lewis, *Semites & Anti-Semites*, 112.

The real problem is threefold. First, the devil rules this planet in his evil way (Luke 4:4–6; 2 Cor. 4:4). Second, the inner culprit, the inborn sinful nature of man (Rom. 5:12), is the source of all our personal troubles and depravity. And third, our own bad decisions account for most of our misfortunes and create self-induced misery (Gal. 6:7–8).[53]

Any effort to blame or eradicate the Jews would only compound our problems and in the end destroy us, as anti-Semitism has destroyed every nation that ever raised a hand against God's people. There is a solution for this innate problem of mankind. This solution begins by simply believing in Christ as your Savior.

> Believe in the Lord Jesus, and you shall be saved. (Acts 16:31b; cf., 2 Cor. 5:17)

Salvation is a free gift of God which one receives "by grace through faith."

> For by grace you have been saved through faith; and that not of yourselves, it is the gift of God; not as a result of works, that no one should boast. (Eph. 2:8–9)

Finally, by learning Bible truths, you grow to spiritual maturity.

> But grow in the grace and knowledge of our Lord and Savior Jesus Christ. (2 Pet. 3:18a)

The result is a biblical perspective of Israel and the Jews' proper place in God's plan.

But remember, there is a vast difference between religion and Christianity. Religion is a system whereby man, by his own efforts and merits, seeks to gain salvation or the approbation of God—an effort doomed to failure.

> As it is written, "There is none righteous, not even one." (Rom. 3:10)

> For all have sinned and fall short of the glory of God. (Rom. 3:23)

Religion persecutes the Jew; biblical Christianity reveres the Jew.

---

53. *Christian Suffering* (1987), 15–17.

Christianity is a personal relationship with God through faith in the person and finished work of Jesus Christ. The Christian cognizant of God's Word knows that anti-Semitism is strictly forbidden (Gen. 12:3; Jer. 12:14; Zech. 12:3; Rom. 11:18–24). Believers must never forget or conveniently overlook the fact that Jesus Christ is a Jew in the royal Davidic line, "the King of Kings and Lord of Lords" (Rev. 19:16). How can anyone worship the Lord God of Israel and at the same time seek the destruction of His people?

God will never honor anti-Semitism. The American, whether believer or unbeliever, who participates in anti-Semitic activities or supports anti-Semitic policies contributes to the decline of the United States.

ANTI-SEMITIC CLAIMS AND THEIR REFUTATION

As a rule, anti-Semitic claims are blanket stereotypical allegations. We have already discussed one such example in the proposition that the Jews are to blame for the world's problems and therefore should be destroyed. Other false statements include: "The Jews are unethical in their business practices and cannot be trusted!" and the ludicrous conspiracy theory "The Jews monopolize and manipulate the international money market!"

Other types of anti-Semitic vituperations are slurs or accusations by innuendo. These vary from derogatory adjectives, coupled with the word "Jew," to a mention of the "Khazars" or a reference to the *Protocols of the Elders of Zion.* These unscrupulous terms claim Jewish duplicity. Just how factual are these claims?

KHAZAR THEORY

Arab countries today have developed a false concept that permeates the teaching of history in Arabic schools and is popularized in their media.[54] This concept proposes that all or nearly all

---

54. Lewis, *Semites & Anti-Semites*, 47–48.

of the ancient Semitic peoples who inhabited the Fertile Crescent, including the Israelites, Canaanites, Phoenicians, Assyrians, and Babylonians, were Arab ancestors.[55] By adopting these Semitic groups, the Arabs lay exclusive claim to all the land of the Middle East. Consequently, Islamic imperial expansion from the seventh century to the present day is justified as a war of liberation to reclaim rightful territory.

This Arab claim could not be disputed were not one of these Semitic peoples still in existence—the Jews. The Jews bear the same name, speak the same language, and profess the same religion as their ancient Israelite ancestors. The Jews who live in Palestine today are definitely *not* Arab forerunners.

There have been various attempts by Arab anti-Semites to whitewash this discrepancy. One hypothesis includes the revival of an old theory that the Jews of Europe are not of true Israelite descent but, instead, are the progeny of the Khazars.[56]

Who were the Khazars? They were semi-nomadic, Tataric in origin, a Turkic-speaking people who first appeared north of the Caucuses in the late second century A.D. In the fifth century they were subjugated by the Huns but rose to power two centuries later. Charging across the Russian steppes, these legendary warriors conquered the Crimea and extended their empire from the western shores of the Caspian Sea to the River Don, from the southern Ukraine to the region north of the Black Sea and as far as Kiev. They fought the Persians and Armenians; they battled Arab expansion, which was inspired by the advent of Islam after the death of Mohammed in 632. In addition, they fought the Byzantine Empire, which forcibly tried to make them Christian.

The "khakan" or ruler was also the religious head of state of the Khazars. Tolerant of other religions, the khakan welcomed thousands of Jews from Asia Minor and the Byzantine Empire as

---

55. The Fertile Crescent, situated between the Arabian Peninsula in the south and the mountains of Armenia in the north, extends from Babylonia up the Tigris and Euphrates rivers to Assyria. From Assyria it continues westward over Syria to the Mediterranean and south to Palestine. Contained in this area are Babylonia, Assyria, Egypt, and Phoenicia.

56. Lewis, *Semites and Anti-Semites*, 48.

well as Mohammedans and Christians. These three religious groups vied to convert the Khazars who practiced a primitive idolatrous religion.

In A.D. 740 after considering the various religious viewpoints among these groups, the khakan embraced Judaism for himself and his people. His conversion was a compromise between Christianity and the religion of Islam. While Judaism was accepted as the official religion of the empire, the Khazar state still maintained tolerance toward other religious groups. The empire continued until A.D. 965 when it was overthrown by a coalition of Christian Russians and the Byzantines.

If the Khazars, not the biblical Israelites, are indeed the ancestors of European Jews, then European Jews have no connection with God's people of the Old Testament, and do not fall under the protective auspices of Genesis 12:1–3. Since European Jews constitute the largest group of immigrants in present day Israel and in the United States, how much easier for anti-Semites to discredit and persecute those whom they consider to be impostors, disconnected with that elect, Old Testament race of people. Anti-Semites sometimes cite this "loophole" to justify their hatred and persecution of Jews. Also, Middle Eastern Arabs can reject the Semitic background of Jewish immigrants to Palestine and thereby preserve the concocted view that gives sanction for conquest of the Land.

The Khazar theory was first proposed by an Austrian anthropologist in the early years of this century. But there is not one shred of evidence to support its validity. Serious scholars have long since abandoned the notion. However, many anti-Semites continue to use the Khazar myth to vindicate their prejudicial racial theories.

PROTOCOLS OF THE ELDERS OF ZION

How did the Jew, long caricatured as the tragicomical, homely peddler, wearing the yellow patch of Jewry, suddenly acquire the image of world conspirator? The concept was first born in the hate-filled imagination of a French Catholic writer by the name of Edouard Drumont in 1886.

Drumont recognized the Jews' intellectual abilities, business acumen, and talent for success; he feared that eventually the Jews would dominate France and Europe by their skillful cunning. Totally disregarding fact or logic, Drumont laid the foundation upon which other anti-Semites would build and expand their fictions against the Jews in France. No doubt his book, *La France Juive* (*The French Jew*), created the clime for the heinous accusation of Captain Dreyfus in 1894.

The Jews, however, did not achieve their present erroneous label as international conspirators until 1903 when a Russian monk, Serge Nilus, published a document entitled *The Protocols of the Elders of Zion*. This book was Nilus' answer to a request from Czar Nicholas II whose psychopathic phobia of the Jews was well-known. The Czar needed "proof" to justify his anti-Semitic sentiments and actions.

Nilus claimed that the book was an exact transcript of a secret meeting held by the elders of Zion in 1897, when they supposedly plotted the disintegration of Christian societies, the instigation of world revolution and wars, and the disruption of education. Since then, *Protocols* has served as the basis for worldwide anti-Semitic propaganda.

The absurdity of the *Protocols* would strain the rationality of all but the most prejudiced person. Does it never occur to those who believe in the veracity of the *Protocols* how unlikely this conglomeration of accusations is? Would the Jews, who are presumedly revealing their own plot, really describe themselves as the agents of evil and do so using the vocabulary of anti-Semitism?

Nilus later admitted that he had forged the documents. However, he also claimed to have acted as "God's instrument" and thought that the *Protocols* should be accepted *as though* they were true. For a while, then, Nicholas II interdicted the publication of the book but it continued to be printed. As had been calculated, *Protocols* sowed the seeds of intense anti-Jewish agitation. During the Bolshevik revolution of 1917, the White Russians revived the *Protocols* to convince the Russian people that the so-called revolution was a Jewish plot to dominate Russia. The result was massacres of Jews during the Russian Civil War and the spread of "the forgery" across Europe. Hitler cited the *Protocols* in his book *Mein Kampf* and neo-Nazis have continued to exploit international conspiracy fears as a plot of the Jews.

Whenever anyone tries to blame the disasters of this world on one collective group of people, the motive is always evil. An entire race cannot be condemned for the actions of a few individuals. Certainly the stage for modern history was set by a number of diabolical international plots. Conspiracies have emerged throughout history, each having central protagonists. These protagonists are not confined to any one race.

What does this prove? Only one thing—*people* are responsible for machinations and plots. Everyone possesses a sin nature (Rom. 3:23), which is the spawning ground for intrigue. But behind every evil international plot is Satan himself (Rev. 12:9).

IMPUGNING JEWISH ETHICS

As for the other claims—unethical business conduct and Jewish monopoly in money matters—these, too, are satanic propaganda. In international money matters, by far the greater proportion of financiers and bankers are Gentiles. Some Jews do lack integrity, but dishonesty exists in every race.

Unfortunately, American society is not immune to these infectious lies. There never has been a Jewish plot in modern history to overthrow the duly established authorities in any nation. And there is no Jewish international conspiracy now. What can be concluded? The Jews are always under attack.

Personal prejudices must not be racially oriented. Because an offensive person happens to be from a certain race that does not make the entire race guilty by association. There are individuals in every ethnic category who are unethical. By the same token there are honorable people in every ethnic group.

No believer in the Lord Jesus Christ can justify being anti-Semitic. God curses and disciplines individuals and groups, including believers, who harbor antagonism toward the Jews. America was founded on biblical principles, one of which is pro-Semitism. Bible teaching, missionary activities, evangelism, and our pro-Semitic policy strengthen our country as a client nation to God.[57]

Our politicians have bartered away our resources, sacrificed principle for expediency, and blundered in so many decisions that by every rule and law—from Bible doctrine to common sense—this country has abused freedom. If anti-Semitism proliferates in America, we will cease to be a nation. Yet we are still here—by the grace of God—and so are the Jews. God still directs history. Conspiracies come and go, but God has never failed to keep His promises. The Jews figure prominently in God's gracious plan. Never forget that fact!

FALSE TEACHING AND ANTI-SEMITISM

Christian beliefs have often been blamed for anti-Semitism— even in America. Let me correct this misconception: *Christian beliefs do not give rise to anti-Semitism; rather ignorance, perversion, and distortion of Christian beliefs spawn anti-Semitism.* Such false teaching must be exposed (Eph. 5:11). Unless we first know the truth, we cannot possibly discern error.

THE CHARGE OF DEICIDE

One of those corrupt beliefs is derived from the erroneous teachings of an early church father by the name of St. John Chrysostom who lived in the fourth century. He charged the Jews with *deicide*—that is, with the "murder of God" in the person of Jesus Christ. Disparagingly, he railed that all Jews, a plague to the world, were hateful to God forever. Therefore, he determined it was God's will that they suffer agony and destruction.

The charge is utterly ridiculous and opens a veritable Pandora's box of heinous crimes against the Jewish people. The term "deicide" is unreasonable and patently false. Any student of Scripture knows there is no greater power than that of sovereign

---

57. A client nation designates a particular relationship of blessing between God and the nation which adheres to these spiritual and establishment principles.

God and that He possesses eternal life (Ps. 90:2). He can neither die nor be put to death by mortal man.

However, the plan of salvation called for the substitutionary death of an innocent, perfect Person in place of guilty sinners. This was clearly portrayed in the Levitical sacrifices (1 Pet. 1:18–20).[58] For this reason the eternal Son of God took on the form of true and sinless humanity. As the God-Man Savior, Jesus Christ came to redeem fallen man from the penalty and power of sin (Isa. 53; cf., 2 Cor. 5:21). His death on the cross could only have occurred with His consent. Who, then, is blameworthy for the crucifixion of Christ?

The Lord's own words cleared the Jews once and for all from the ludicrous charge of deicide. He declared:

> I am the good shepherd; the good shepherd lays down His life for the sheep . . . I lay down my life . . . *No one has taken it away from me, but I lay it down on my own initiative.* I have authority to lay it down, and I have authority to take it up again. This commandment I received from my Father. (John 10:11, 17, 18, italics added)

The Jews are not the "Christ-killers" whom the anti-Semites would have them be. Although many Jews rejected Jesus as the Messiah, only a small faction—the religious leaders in Jerusalem, the chief priest, and the Pharisees—actually plotted His death (Matt. 26:3–5; John 11:46–53). Still others, those average citizens in Roman-occupied Judea, believed in Him (John 11:45), the faith response which determined their eternal future.

> For God so loved the world, that He gave His only begotten [uniquely born] Son, that whoever believes in Him should not perish, but have eternal life. For God did not send the Son into the world to judge the world; but that the world should be saved through Him. He who believes in Him is not judged; he who does not believe has been judged already, because he has not

---

58. *Levitical Offerings* (1973), 10–30.

believed in the name of the only begotten [uniquely born] Son of God. (John 3:16–18)

Under the law of culpability as stated in Deuteronomy 24:16, Jeremiah 31:29–30, and Ezekiel 18:2, fathers could not be held liable, penalized, or blamed for the sins of their children, nor children for the sins of their fathers. Rather, each person is held accountable for his own sins. Thus, the oft quoted cry of the conspirators, "His [Christ's] blood be upon us, and on our children" (Matt. 27:25), no more invoked an eternal curse on all Jewry than the figurative hand washing ritual of Pilate absolved him from passing the death sentence on Jesus Christ, a man he knew to be totally innocent (Matt. 27:24). The Jewish religious leaders immediately involved with the crucifixion were merely sealing their own doom, not pronouncing an eternal curse on all Jews.

Seeing that Pilate could be manipulated, the seeds of rebellion were sown and Israel's destruction insured. In A.D. 63, thousands of restive Jews would be crucified on that very spot, and in A.D. 70 an even greater tragedy would overtake them. In the siege and destruction of Jerusalem they would suffer over a million casualties.[59]

Does the blame for the crucifixion rest on Pontius Pilate? Again, only in the sense that he was culpable for his own decision. Pilate had interrogated Jesus and had found Him above reproach (John 18:38; 19:4, 6). Yet Pilate lacked the moral courage necessary to back up his conviction. His investigation, which proved Christ innocent of any crime, offered Pilate the best reason not to pronounce the death penalty. But given to vacillation, Pilate sought a compromise solution to placate the hostile religious leaders. He feared the implications of their threat,

If you release this Man, you are no friend of Caesar. (John 19:12*b*)

Admittedly, Pilate had boasted of his authority and power to

---

59. Josephus, "The Wars of the Jews," Book VI, ix.

either crucify Jesus or set Him free (John 19:10). Yet Jesus clarified the issue by His statement:

> You would have no authority over Me, unless it had been given you from above. (John 19:11*a*)

Pilate was in a quandary. God in His omniscience knew Pilate's dilemma and used it to bring His Son to the cross. Therefore, Jesus completed His answer to Pilate by stating, "For this reason he who delivered Me up to you has the greater sin" (John 19:11*b*).

Obviously Jesus was referring not to God the Father who had "delivered Him [Jesus] up for us all" (Rom. 8:32). God cannot sin. Rather, Jesus was indicting one person—the high priest, Caiaphas (John 18:24, 28–29). The magnitude of Caiaphas' sin lay first of all in his rejection of Jesus Christ and, secondly, in his ruthless use of others—Pilate, the Roman soldiers, the incited, howling mob—to carry out his evil design (John 16:2).

Yet Caiaphas' treachery, Pilate's decision based on political expediency, the vicious plot of the Sanhedrin,[60] as well as the role of the Roman soldiers who carried out the execution, were all exonerated when Jesus prayed,

> "Father, forgive them; for they do not know what they are doing." (Luke 23:34)

To these words, the Apostle Paul adds,

> "For had they known [Him], they would not have crucified the Lord of glory." (1 Cor. 2:8; cf., Acts 13:27)

The Bible concludes that all members of the human race are sinners (Rom. 3:23). As sinners, we cannot meet the perfect standards of God. We are totally incapable of meeting our debt (Isa. 64:6; Titus 3:5). Jesus Christ met that obligation for us. One purpose only sent Him to the cross—to bear the sins of the entire

---

60. The Sanhedrin was a governing assembly composed of high priests (the acting high priest, those who had been high priests, and members of the privileged families from which the high priests were taken), elders (tribal and family heads of the people and priesthood), and scribes (legal assessors), Pharisees, and Sadducees. See *Unger's Bible Dictionary*, 1976 ed., s.v. "Sanhedrin."

human race. There, hanging between heaven and earth, Christ was judged for those sins and our debt was canceled (Col. 2:14).

We all share the sinner's condemnation, as well as the offer of salvation (Rom. 6:23). It amounts to this:

> Where sin increased, grace abounded all the more. (Rom. 5:20)

God the Father's love compelled Him to sacrifice His Son. Christ's love for mankind compelled Him to endure the agony and humiliation of the cross (Rom. 5:8; cf., Heb. 12:2). In love the Holy Spirit reveals the plan of salvation to the unbeliever (John 16:8–11). The crucifixion is not a matter of murder but of grace, for the cross was God's provision for man's sinfulness long before man was created.

COVENANT VERSUS DISPENSATIONAL THEOLOGY

Unfortunately, incorrect Bible teaching is not limited to the early Church alone. One branch of current orthodox theology, which leaves the door ajar to anti-Semitism, is Covenant Theology. In contrast to Dispensationalism, Covenant Theology blurs the distinction between Israel and the Church, denying Israel as a nation the fulfillment of the unconditional covenants promised by God. While no reputable Covenant theologian derives anti-Semitism from this view, some Christians could possibly misconstrue covenant tenets as a basis for anti-Semitism.

Covenant theologians perceive Israel not as a racial and national entity to whom God made unconditional promises, but as a spiritual (regenerate) people of God.[61] Since Israel disobeyed God, Covenant theologians contend that the Church assumes the role as "spiritual Israel." Thus, the Church, which began as a remnant of Old Testament believers, is continuous with true Israel. The unconditional covenants originally given to Israel are now transferred to the new spiritual people, the Church. In his *Systematic Theology* Dr. Lewis Sperry Chafer writes:

---

61. For a delineation of the difference between racial and regenerate (true) Israel see Chapter 6, below.

> The Covenant Theory does retain Israel as such to the time of Christ's death. The Church is thought to be a spiritual remnant within Israel to whom all Old Testament blessings are granted and the nation as such is allowed to inherit the cursings.[62]

This final premise is fraught with potential anti-Semitism. It denies that the Jews have a national future and overlooks the obvious reference to Israel in the biblical promise:

> God has not rejected His people whom He foreknew. (Rom. 11:2*a*)

If spiritual (regenerate or true) Israel, not national Israel, were the only recipient of the Genesis 12:3 promise of preservation, and if the Church is now "spiritual Israel," then the anti-Semitism clause no longer protects unregenerate Jews. Based on this view, Christians might indeed find an excuse to blame and persecute Jews for a myriad of problems. Furthermore, to interpret the term "Israel" in the New Testament as exclusively signifying "spiritual Israel," meaning the Church, disavows that the word can have other meanings in context.[63]

At the Second Advent of Jesus Christ true Israel in contrast to the Church will enter into the fulfillment of the unconditional covenants (Rom. 9:6–7). Throughout Israel's history there was always a requirement of faith in *Yahweh* for individual Israelites to become true Israel (Gen. 15:6; cf., Rom. 4:1–3). But this regenerate Israel was still part of the nation. In the Millennium the entire nation, regenerate and unregenerate, will benefit from the physical aspects of the unconditional covenants—the Land, a king, and

---

62. L.S. Chafer, *Systematic Theology*, 8 vols. (Dallas: Dallas Seminary Press, 1948), 4:311.

63. Scripture uses terms like "Israel," "Jew," "seed of Abraham," and "chosen people" in at least four senses: (1) The biological descendants of Abraham (Rom. 9—11); (2) the political sense (Jer. 3:11); (3) a spiritual sense that applies to any individual or group regardless of racial background who are regenerate, i.e. the spiritual sense may be used to distinguish mere biological Jews from Jews who are both biologically and spiritually related to God as in Romans 4:6ff.; and (4) a typological sense. See John S. Feinberg, ed., *Continuity and Discontinuity* (Westchester, Illinois: Crossway Books, 1988), 72.

blessing—but the unregenerate cannot receive the eternal aspects of the covenants. Regenerate Israel was the catalyst for Old Testament prophecies that depict a future for Israel as a nation.

The New Testament never confuses Israel and the Church. Even though the Age of Israel and the Church Age share in God's grace way of salvation, this fact alone does not constitute *proof* that the Church is now "spiritual Israel." The Church did not originate in Abraham's tent but on the day of Pentecost. The book of Acts, which describes characteristics unique to the beginnings of the Church, also delineates obvious uses of the term Israel in the national sense in order to maintain the difference between the two entities (Acts 3:12; 4:10; 5:21; 21:28). When Peter spoke to the "Men of Israel" in Acts 2:22 he was alluding to ethnic Jews not to the Church. Likewise, when Paul addressed "my kinsmen according to the flesh" (Rom. 9:3–4), he was speaking to racial Jews. And the Israelite congregation of Acts 7:38 was never included in the New Testament Church.

To assert that regenerate Israel throughout its history is equivalent to the Church is to miscalculate the uniqueness of the Church. One cannot undervalue references in Scripture to the "Mystery Age"—the Church (Eph. 3:8–10)—as well as to the changes brought about by the coming of the Holy Spirit (Acts 1:5, 8; Acts 2).[64]

Dispensational Theology exposes the shortcomings of Covenant Theology. Even though today the dispensational interpretation of the Bible is increasingly ridiculed, Dispensational Theology holds the key to understanding the Scriptures in their proper perspective. Dispensationalism clarifies the difference between Israel and the Church and defines the Christian's modus operandi and his relationships.

Israel was founded ethnically with Abraham (Gen. 12:2) and nationally with Moses (Ex. 3:8–10; cf., 19:5–6). This Jewish Age continued up to the time of Jesus Christ.[65] Interrupted by the Church Age, the Jewish era resumes after the Rapture of the

---

64. A "mystery" in the New Testament is something that was previously hidden but is now revealed (Rom. 16:25; 1 Cor. 2:7, 10).

65. See *The Divine Outline of History*, 29–30.

Church and terminates seven years later with the Second Advent of the Lord.

There are startling differences between these two dispensations. In the Age of Israel, there was a specialized priesthood, the Levitical Priesthood (Num. 18:1, 2, 8). The enduement or empowerment of the Holy Spirit was limited to only a few believers such as rulers, judges, priests, artisans of the Tabernacle, or builders of the Temple, but these believers could lose the Holy Spirit through persistent carnality (Ps. 51:11; cf., 1 Sam. 16:14). Another outstanding characteristic of the Jewish Age was Israel's sole custodianship of God's Word (Rom. 3:1–2). One nation was responsible for the dissemination of the Gospel and scriptural truth (Isa. 43:10–12).

In 445 B.C., dating from the decree by Artaxerxes Longimanus (Neh. 2:1–8) to restore and build Jerusalem, the Jews were promised 490 more years to evangelize other nations (Dan. 9:24–26). The term "seventy weeks" used by Daniel refers to a literal period of 490 years. However, seven years short of the time allotted to them for this particular operation, the cross occurred— Messiah was "cut off" as prophesied in Daniel 9:26—and the Jewish Age was halted. But God still owes Israel seven more years, and He will keep that promise during the Tribulation, a period called in Scripture the "time of Jacob's distress" or that "seventieth week" of Daniel 9.

The Church Age is the present dispensation on the divine timetable. In the Church Age, the Royal Family, a holy nation, a chosen race, called the "Church," made up of every born-again believer, Jew or Gentile, (1 Pet. 2:9; cf., Rom. 10:12; Gal. 3:28), assumes unique responsibilities in the plan of God.

The universal Church is an organism, not a national organization. Regardless of the nation or geographical location in which the believer resides, every one now is a member of the "body" (1 Cor. 12:12ff), a royal priest (1 Pet. 2:5), and an ambassador for the absent Christ (Rom. 1:14–16; 2 Cor. 5:18–20). Every member of the Royal Family is permanently indwelled by the Holy Spirit (John 14:16; 1 Cor. 6:19–20) and has the completed Canon of

Scripture, as well as unique divine operating assets.[66] While on earth, the Church is called the "Body of Christ" (Eph. 5:23); in heaven, the Church becomes the "Bride of Christ" (2 Cor. 11:2; Rev. 19:6–8). The Church is God's heavenly people (Heb. 12:22–23); Israel is God's earthly people (Deut. 14:2; Isa. 66:22). Israel walked by sight (Ex. 4:30; Ps. 78:12; 1 Cor. 1:22); the Church walks by faith (2 Cor. 5:7).

Unless these distinctions between Israel and the Church are maintained, a believer cannot orient to the Christian life—a supernatural way of life, executed in the filling of the Holy Spirit, which includes a proper attitude and respect for the Jews. To blur these distinctions is to cause confusion, and "God is not a God of confusion" (1 Cor. 14:33). The blurred distinctions are the danger of the erroneous teaching of Covenant Theology.

The entire Bible and the structure of Christianity depend on recognizing that God made four unconditional covenants with Israel—not with the Church. Either God must keep His covenant with the nation Israel to whom He made the promise or He is false to His Word, which is unthinkable and blasphemous (Num. 23:19). The covenant theologian's position in amalgamating Israel and the Church denigrates the character of God and cannot be supported by Scripture. The Jews have a national future and will always be very much a part of the plan of God.

BRITISH ISRAELITISM

When the Word of God is not accurately taught, spiritual growth declines and apostasy prevails. One form of this apostasy is "British Israelitism." Found in a variety of churches, the insidious fellowship adroitly proclaims a garbled version of prophecy. Driven by a similar motivation as the adherents of the Khazar myth, the followers of British Israelitism seek to discredit Jewish origins. They too perpetrate the fiction that the Jewish race today is not descended from Abraham. With a baffling mixture of Scripture

---

66. *The Divine Outline of History*, 80–141.

taken out of context and spurious historical claims, they argue that the Anglo-Saxon people are the true Israel, and thus, the recipients of the unconditional covenants.

Followers of British Israelitism allege that when the Southern Kingdom of Judah fell in 586 B.C., Zedekiah's daughters (Jer. 41:10) escaped death by fleeing to Egypt (Jer. 44:12–14) and then found refuge (Isa. 37:31–32) with Jeremiah sailing to one of the "isles of the sea" (Jer. 31:10). The "isles" were Ireland and later England where these Israelites became the royal house of England.[67]

But this royal linkage is not the only fabricated connection between Anglo-Saxons and Israel. They also allege that commoners among Anglo-Saxon people in England, Germany, Holland, and other European lands are descended from the ten lost tribes of Israel. Presumably this refers to the ten tribes of the Northern Kingdom who were taken into captivity in 721 B.C. British Israelites claim that these tribes wandered across Europe, filtered through many nations (Amos 9:9), and eventually settled in England.

British Israelites pride themselves in being the progeny of the ten lost tribes of Israel. These mixed up Gentiles insist that the ancient Israelites were not Semites; therefore, Jews today, all of whom are Semites, must be excluded from the genealogy of Israel. They deny the Jews their rightful place in God's plan for the nation Israel. They claim for themselves, as the Anglo-Saxon descendants of the ancient Israelites, the blessings of the unconditional covenants. As proof of this theory, British Israelites extol the historical blessings accorded to Anglo-Saxon culture that culminated in the rise of the British Empire. These blessings, in contrast to the hideous persecutions that have plagued the Jews for centuries, confirm their status as the elect race.

This entire scenario is utter nonsense.

Close scrutiny of the hermeneutics employed in interpreting various texts of Scripture that British Israelites use to bolster their racial theory reveals untenable exegetical methods. Likewise, no

---

67. *Evangelical Dictionary of Theology*, 1984 ed., s.v. "British Israelitism," by I. Hexam.

creditable historian supports the racial and national arguments made by this group.[68]

Only a few scattered groups of dedicated British Israelites remain in the United States. But their influence is to be found in somewhat distorted form in publications like Herbert W. Armstrong's *The Plain Truth*.[69] An even more sinister group, a pseudo-Christian movement called "Identity churches," has incorporated these false teachings into a more virile guise. These so-called "churches" are essentially hate-mongers that promote the superiority of the white race. They 'identify' themselves as "true Israel," Aryans, white Anglo-Saxons. Relentless vilification of the Jews and racial bigotry are the cornerstones of their blasphemous "theology."

British Israelites also contend that as David's offspring they have the same spiritual responsibilities as their ancestors. What are these responsibilities? They must keep the Sabbath and the Ten Commandments. They must adhere to the "kosher" (dietary) food regulations imposed under the Mosaic Law for the Israelites' safety. They must observe the Passover and other holy days.

What does the Scripture say? The dietary laws of the Old Testament were set aside after the Church Age began (Acts 10:9–16) and are no longer an issue (1 Cor. 10:23–33). The special feast days are now defunct and the Christian is to consider each day alike as a grace gift from God (Rom. 14:6).

While British Israelites are prone to blame the problems of the world on the Khazars or Jews in general, they blame the troubles of America and Britain on failure to comply with the Decalogue and on the worship of materialism rather than the worship of God. Undoubtedly our nation is deteriorating because principles of divine establishment, morality, and spirituality are rejected by increasing numbers of our citizens. There is no new morality, only the old immorality disguised in modern garb.

The Ten Commandments are a summary of divine mandates pertaining to freedom, protection of life, liberty, and property of

68. *Ibid.*
69. *Ibid.*

a specific national entity, Israel. However, when any nation operates under the principle of divine establishment, not only individual freedom and happiness but national stability and prosperity result. Where these commandments and accompanying principles are constantly violated by a majority of a population, that nation is headed for disaster.

Nevertheless, while the United States was founded upon these fundamental truths, Mosaic legislation was *never* given to anyone but the Jews (Ex. 19:3; Lev. 26:46). The Law was never intended for the Gentiles (Deut. 4:8). Jesus Christ fulfilled the Law in every detail (Matt. 5:17), and now that Law is abrogated for the Church (Rom. 6:14; 10:4; Gal. 2:19).[70] Since Christ is the end of the Law where believers of the Church Age are concerned, the Christian, both Jew and Gentile, is subject to a higher law—the "law of the Spirit of life in Christ Jesus" (Rom. 8:2–4; 1 Cor. 13; Gal. 5:18, 22–23).

Sad to note, yet typical of our day, many succumb and blindly accept man-made gimmicks and false gospels while readily rejecting the truths of the Word of God. The pernicious effects are evident in the subjective thinking of the present generation. The fact remains no one can walk with one foot in the Law and the other in grace.

To know the difference, the Scriptures must be exegeted in the light of dispensational truths and in the context in which they were written. Therefore, when anyone claims that the Jews today are not descendants of Abraham, avoid them; separate yourself from apostasy in obedience to Second Corinthians 6:17, Second Thessalonians 3:14–15, and Second Timothy 3:5.

---

70. See *The Divine Outline of History*, 33–35, 57–58.

5

The Biblical View of Anti-Semitism

THE AUTHOR OF ANTI-SEMITISM

THE ANNALS OF HISTORY prove conclusively that anti-Semitism is a masterstroke of evil genius. The author and sponsor is that phenomenal prehistoric supercreature, Lucifer, who was renamed Satan in his fallen state. Anti-Semitism is one of the primary weapons used in his attempts to usurp the plan of God. As the absolute commander of all fallen angels (Matt. 9:34; 12:26), comprising one-third of the heavenly host (Rev. 12:4), he has thrown his entire organization into the conflict (Eph. 6:10–12). His rulership over this planet (Luke 4:5–7; Eph. 2:2) gives him the distinct advantage of being able to manipulate the nations of this world (Rev. 12:9; 20:3, 8). One of his foremost strategies is to annihilate the people who figure so prominently in God's design—the Jews.

The success of that strategy is self-evident. Satan's cleverness can be seen in the gullibility of otherwise intelligent people who readily swallow the devil's colossal lies regarding the Jews. Another confirmation is the intense persecution of the Jews by a broad assortment of peoples, the likes of which no other race in history has experienced. Yet another indicator is the constant agitation by the Arabs, the half-brothers of the Jews. The Arabs have long been in dispute with the Jews over the ownership of the promised Land.

Yet these are not the only manifestations where the prince of darkness influences the affairs of this world. The very fact that anti-Semitism also afflicts some believers is an additional triumph for satanic strategy. For those who have no anti-Semitic tendencies, he has alternate plans. One of his obvious objectives is the destruction of the focus in the Christian life—Bible doctrine. If the believer is ignorant of Bible doctrine and does not know his enemy, he easily becomes a casualty of this spiritual warfare.

By appealing to human arrogance, by suggesting temporal solutions to problems only God can solve, by advocating human crusades designed to improve the devil's world, Satan seeks to divert the believer's attention, purpose, and energies from spiritual growth. Thus, the believer is rendered ineffective in the angelic conflict, and Satan scores another tactical victory.

Cleverly substituting religion for the truth of the Word of God, the devil blinds unbelievers to the Gospel (2 Cor. 4:3–4) and distracts believers from the Christian way of life (1 Tim. 5:15). By opposing Bible doctrine and sponsoring rebellion against divinely established law and order, Satan attempts to fulfill his purpose of making himself "like the Most High" (Isa. 14:13–14). To this end he encourages revolt against God, but never against himself.

Recent trends in the United States illustrate the fascination with the powers of darkness. Never before in our history have Americans been so preoccupied with Satanism, the occult, witchcraft, and mysticism. Drug addiction and dabbling in demonism have opened the door to Satan-worship with all its attendant evils. Animal and even human sacrifices have become increasingly prevalent and more blatant, as Satan's adherents attempt to glorify "the god of this world" (2 Cor. 4:4). Tarot cards and the Ouija board vie with astrology charts and palm readers for the attention of those who never before went beyond seeking their future in a fortune cookie.

No wonder "a deluding influence" (2 Thess. 2:11) threatens the very fabric of our nation. Satan knows that a deluded people are a neutralized people. Now, if he can persuade the United States to continue its drift toward anti-Semitism, so much the better; we would cease to be a client nation to God.

Why should Satan purposely cause upheaval and turmoil in his own domain? For a simple reason: so he can offer a bewildered world longing for peace nebulous visions of a utopian future, which can only be established by Christ at His Second Advent. To accomplish this goal, every wicked means to that end is justified. In Satan's opinion, one of the most efficient strategies for securing his domain would be the elimination of Jewry.

Satanic antagonism against the Jews is well documented throughout the Old Testament and is predicted in the New Testament. Only the methods vary—never the objective. The devil's initial purpose was to foil the coming of Christ into the world by destroying the lines of Adam, Abraham, and David. After Christ was born, Satan's subsequent goal was to hinder Jesus from going to the cross. He failed at this as well: Now his aim is to prevent the Lord's second coming to rescue the Jews and set up the millennial kingdom.

During the present dispensation as Satan's time grows short, the angelic conflict is greatly intensified. His frustration and fury is unleashed primarily against the Royal Family—the Church. Secondarily, Satan's attack involves violent outbursts of anti-Semitism. However, none of these waves of anti-Semitism can compare to the persecutions which are yet to come when the Church is removed as the primary target, and the restraining ministry of the Holy Spirit is also removed.

SATANIC STRATEGY TO HINDER THE PLAN OF GOD

A brief survey of Satan's strategic attempts to reach his objectives depicts his unrelenting hatred of God and His chosen people. More than that, Satan's failure proves God's eternal faithfulness in preserving His own and perpetuating His plan.

1. The attack on Adam's seed (Gen. 3:15)
   a. The murder of Abel, accomplished through Satan's indwelling of Cain (Gen. 4:8; cf., 1 John 3:12)
      God's counterattack: substitution of Seth (Gen. 4:25); the Messianic line perpetuated (Luke 3:23, 38)
   b. The angelic infiltration to corrupt the human race (Gen. 6:1–13)
      God's counterattack: the flood and preservation of Noah and his family (Gen. 6:7; 8:1)

2. The attack on Abraham's seed
   a. Sarah taken to Pharaoh's harem (Gen. 12:10–16)
      God's counterattack: Sarah delivered by the Lord's intervention (Gen. 12:17–20)
   b. Pharaoh's command to murder all Hebrew male infants (Ex. 1:15–16)
      God's counterattack: the birth and preservation of Moses (Ex. 2:1–10)
   c. Pharaoh's attempted destruction of the Israelites at the Red Sea (Ex. 14:5–12)
      God's counterattack: the destruction of Pharaoh and his forces (Ex. 14:26–28)

3. The attack on David's seed
   a. Jehoram's murder of his royal brothers (2 Chron. 21:1–5)
      God's counterattack: Philistine and Arab invaders seize and sell Jehoram's family into slavery; youngest son, Jehoahaz, preserved (2 Chron. 21:16–17)
   b. Athaliah's murder of the royal seed (2 Chron. 22:10)
      God's counterattack: the rescue of Joash (2 Chron. 22:11–12); Athaliah executed (2 Chron. 23:10–15)
   c. Hezekiah left childless and near death at a time when Assyria threatened war (Isa. 36:1)
      God's counterattack: the destruction of the Assyrians (Isa. 37:36–37); Hezekiah's life extended (Isa. 38); royal line promised (Isa. 39:7)

4. Haman's plot to exterminate all Jews in the Persian Empire (Esth. 3:6ff)

God's counterattack: the Jews delivered (Esth. 7); Haman and anti-Semites executed (Esth. 7:10ff)

5. The attack on Joseph's seed (Matt. 1:16), the legal line to the throne of David
   a. Mary's pregnancy and Joseph's nobility (Matt. 1:18–19; cf., Deut. 22:14, 20–21; 24:1)
      God's counterattack: divine revelation and instructions (Matt. 1:20–25)
   b. Herod's command for the slaying of infants (Matt. 2:16–18)
      God's counterattack: divine revelation and instructions to flee to Egypt (Matt. 2:13)

6. The attacks on Christ during His Incarnation
   a. The satanic temptations in the desert (Matt. 4:1–10; Luke 4:1–12)
   b. The attempts to stone Jesus (John 8:59; 10:30–39)
   c. The temptation to forego the cross (John 12:27; Luke 22:39–44)
   d. The attempts to kill Jesus before He reached the cross (Matt. 27:26, 29–30; Mark 14:65; 15:15, 19; Luke 22:63–64)
   e. The temptation to come down from the cross (Matt. 27:40–44; cf., Matt. 26:53–54)
      God's counterattack: the strengthening of Jesus Christ (Matt. 4:11; Luke 22:43); the Father's reassurance (John 12:28); the Son's determination to obey the Father's will (John 12:27; 17:4; 19:30); the Son's sustenance by the Holy Spirit (Luke 4:1) and doctrine (Ps. 31:5)

7. The attack on the Word of God (Gen. 3:1; Luke 8:12; 2 Cor. 4:4)
   God's counterattack: the preservation of the Canon despite every effort toward its destruction (Matt. 24:35; cf., Isa. 40:8; 1 Pet. 1:25)

8. The attack on the Royal Family (Eph. 6:12; 1 Pet. 5:8)
   God's counterattack: combat-readiness and strengthening in the intensified stage of the angelic conflict (Eph. 6:10–18; 1 Pet. 5:7–10; 1 John 4:4)

9. The attack on Israel in the Tribulation (Dan. 12:1; cf., Matt. 24:4–26; Rev. 12—13)
   God's counterattack: the deliverance of the Jews at the Second Advent of Christ (Joel 2:20ff; 3:16; Zech. 14:2–9, 11) and destruction of their enemies (Zech. 9:14–15; 14:12–14; Rev. 19:21); incarceration of Satan (Rev. 20:1–3)

10. The Gog and Magog rebellion (Rev. 20:7–8)
    God's counterattack: the annihilation of the last revolutionaries (Rev. 20:9); Satan's final judgment (Rev. 20:10)

ANTI-SEMITISM AND THE ANGELIC CONFLICT

Anti-Semitism, like so many other trends in history, is simply a fallout from the angelic conflict, which has raged since "before the foundation of the world." If Satan has any remaining hope to emerge victorious in this conflict of the ages, this hope hinges on the destruction of the Jews. Were he successful in wiping out every trace of Jewry from the face of the earth, God would find no Jews to deliver nor could He fulfill His national promises to Israel; hence, the Second Advent could not occur.

We know from Scripture that angelic convocations are held periodically in heaven to consider historical trends (Job 1:6–12; 2:1–7; Zech. 3:1–7). Therefore, man is under close scrutiny by both elect and fallen angels (1 Cor. 4:9). We also know that Satan as the ruler of the world and Jesus Christ as the One who controls human history both influence earthly events, with our Lord always having the sovereign power to overrule the machinations of Satan (Ps. 33:10–19; 135:5–6) and preserve mankind.

As the author of evil in this world, including anti-Semitism, Satan has tried from the first appearance of Jews in history to eradicate them in the most devious ways. Never has one race been the target of such animosity and terrible persecutions; yet the Jews have survived their tormentor. According to God's promise there will never be a generation in human history without a representation of Jews, regenerate or unregenerate. Every time you see a Jew you should be reminded of God's faithfulness. Satan may be the ruler of this planet, but even he can accomplish only what God permits. Anti-Semitism is of the devil and can never fully succeed.

The principle that Satan is the author of anti-Semitism is delineated in Revelation 12. Here the past and future of this great evil are clearly depicted and described by the Apostle John:

> And a great sign appeared in heaven: a woman clothed with the sun, and the moon under her feet, and on her head a crown of twelve stars. (Rev. 12:1)

Verse 1 introduces a vision of a woman clothed in dazzling garments composed of the sun, the moon, and twelve stars. Who is she? What does all this signify?

Scripture always explains Scripture; this is a law of hermeneutics, or textual interpretation. Once before, the sun, moon, and stars appeared together as a part of a divine revelation. It was in Joseph's prophetic dream (Gen. 37:5, 9ff). That dream concerned the Jews, as does this particular sign. In the Genesis narrative Joseph's father, Jacob, was instantly aware to whom these heavenly bodies referred. He soundly reprimanded Joseph by saying,

> What is this dream that you have had? Shall I and your mother and your brothers actually come to bow ourselves down before you to the ground? (Gen. 37:10*b*)

The "sun," therefore, represents Jacob; the "moon," his wives Rachel and Leah; and "the crown of twelve stars" symbolizes his brothers, the twelve patriarchs of Israel. Taken together they portray the Jewish people, who will always exist on the earth.

The woman in the sign is Mary, and she is shown in her relationship to Israel as a descendant of Jacob's line. Mary could trace her lineage—the royal blood line to the throne—to the house of Judah through Nathan, son of David and Bathsheba (Luke 3:31–34); her husband, Joseph, descended from the legal line through Solomon (Matt. 1:4). Both lines had crossed. This sign spans the centuries, from the time of Jacob and the patriarchs to the "fulness of the time" (Gal. 4:4) and introduces the promised Savior.

And she was with child; and she cried out, being in
labor and in pain to give birth. (Rev. 12:2)

God chose Mary to bring Messiah into the world. He is the seed
of the woman of Genesis 3:15 and was supernaturally conceived by
the virgin Mary through the agency of the Holy Spirit (Isa. 7:14;
cf., Luke 1:30–35). Revelation 12:2 projects a dramatic moment
from the past as though it were about to occur: the virgin birth of
Jesus Christ.

In this birth, as in all others, there is intense pain (Gen. 3:16).
Consequently, the woman screams out as the labor pains rack her
body. This meaning is conveyed by the Greek verb *krazo*. Labor
pains will always be a reality and will occur at intervals until the
child is delivered.

Now the scene changes:

And another sign appeared in heaven: and behold, a
great red dragon, having seven heads and ten horns, and
on his head were seven diadems. (Rev. 12:3)

The second sign presents the archenemy, Satan, in symbolic form
as the "great red dragon." The term "dragon" was first used by
Homer and Aeschylus. *Drakon* in the Greek is derived from the
verb *derkomai*, which means "to see clearly, to have perspicacity."
Superior intelligence and foresight aptly describe the devil's assets
which have enabled him to deceive nations and peoples on the
earth as he once deceived the woman in the Garden.

WORLD EMPIRES AND ANTI-SEMITISM

His appearance is awesome. The present tense of *echo*, meaning
"to have and to hold," depicts Satan as having "seven heads." Six
of those heads review a section of history and refer to the six
great empires which in the past attacked and sought to destroy
Israel. They include Egypt, Assyria, Babylon, Medo-Persia, Graeco-
Macedonia, and Rome. With the exception of Egypt, all these
nations once administered severe discipline to the Jews. Just as
God "spanks" His children on an individual basis when they step

out of line (Heb. 12:6), so God used these empires to discipline
Israel for the same purpose.[71]

Egypt originally enslaved the Jews during the reigns of Thutmose
I and Amenhotep II. A thousand years later Assyria administered
the fifth cycle of discipline to the Northern Kingdom in 721 B.C.
and simultaneously the fourth cycle to the Southern Kingdom.
Babylon, later known as Chaldea, completely devastated Judah in
586 B.C. and carried the survivors into captivity. Medo-Persia
sponsored the return of the Jews to their native land and extended
benevolent treatment toward them. But a later king, Xerxes I, a
duped anti-Semite, tried to destroy the Jews.

Graeco-Macedonia was also kindly disposed toward the Jews in
the beginning. Yet later Hellenistic monarchies under the Ptolemies
and the Seleucids turned against Jewry. In A.D. 70 Rome
dispensed the fifth cycle of discipline to Judah. This began the
present dispersion of the Jews and the prophetic judgment of
Leviticus 26:27–39 and Deuteronomy 28:47–62 was fulfilled for the
last time. Thus these past empires, at one time or another, were
willing tools in the attempted annihilation of the Jews.

Represented as the seventh crown and the ten horns in
Revelation 12:3, the final empire dispenses the last vial of intensified anti-Semitism against the Jew. The ten horns are a confederation of nations, the future Revived Roman Empire.[72] These are the
"feet and toes" nations in the image of Daniel 2:41–45 and are
identical to the satanic organization of Revelation 17:12–13. John
describes this confederation as:

> the beast that . . . was [the Imperial Rome of his day,
> in A.D. 96] and is not [no longer in existence after A.D.
> 476], and is about to come up out of the abyss

---

71. When Israel was saturated with apostasy, the Jews were warned through the
increasing intensity of four cycles of discipline (Lev. 26). Verses 14–17 describe the
first cycle; verses 18–20, the second cycle; verses 21–22, the third cycle; and verses
23–26, the fourth cycle. The fifth cycle (verses 27–39) ends in military defeat and
the destruction of the nation (Jer. 7:24–34). See *Daniel: Chapters One, Two, &
Three*, (1988), 45.

72. See footnote 19, page 9 above.

[sponsored by Satan in the Tribulation] and to go to destruction [at the close of Armageddon]. (Rev. 17:8*a*)

However, before vanishing forever from history, the Revived Roman Empire will contribute immeasurably to the suffering of both Christians and Jews.

But before that future anti-Semitism is detailed, Revelation 12:4–5 continues to look at the past. In the first half of verse 4 the prehistoric events, which followed Lucifer's rebellion, are summarized and the removal of the fallen angels from heaven is confirmed:

> And his [Satan's] tail swept away a third of the stars of heaven [angelic creatures who followed Satan at his first fall], and threw them to the earth. (Rev. 12:4*a*)

The angelic conflict is still a heavenly conflict, although repercussions have extended to planet earth since the creation of mankind. There will come a time when all fallen angels will be evicted from heaven and exiled to the earth. That expulsion will take place in the middle of the Tribulation.

SATAN'S ULTIMATE DEFEAT

The distant future and prehistoric past merge into a single occurrence in John's era—the virgin birth of Jesus Christ.

> And the dragon stood [with antagonism] before the woman [Mary] who was about to give birth, so that when she gave birth he might devour her child [Jesus]. (Rev. 12:4*b*)

Because Satan fully comprehends that Jesus as the Messiah was the fulfillment of Genesis 3:15 and the beginning of his end, he assumed the position of adversary of the Jew from the time of Abraham to the very moment of the Incarnation. He tried his utmost to cut off the Messianic line. Often only one surviving member of the royal lineage remained to fulfill God's plan. Yet God faithfully preserved the line of Christ, and Satan's fiendish strategy failed.

Satan was again present to frustrate the coming of the One who was both the Son of God and the Son of Man. This personal attack was concentrated against the greatest of all Jews, the Lord Jesus Christ. Imagine the devil's impotent fury when he realized that he could no more hinder the First Advent than he could destroy the ancestry of Jesus.

> And she gave birth to a son, a male child, who is to rule all the nations with a rod of iron; and her child was caught up to God and to His throne. (Rev. 12:5)

The futuristic present infinitive of *poimaino*, "to rule," states the certainty of Christ's millennial reign as the Shepherd of Israel, while the reference to the "rod of iron" indicates the absolute justice of His rule. The concept of the first strategic victory in the angelic conflict is couched in terms of the "catching up" of the child to God and His throne.[73]

During the entire thirty-three-and-a-half years that our Lord was on the earth, Satan constantly opposed Him by throwing temptations into His path and instigating assassination plots. Yet God provided the needed power and protection for Jesus to fulfill His purpose. To triumph over Satan, the Savior must go to the cross, bear the sins of the world (1 John 2:2), and be judged in our place (1 Pet. 2:24; cf., 1 John 3:8). He did so as the sinless Son of God, because He is undiminished deity—equal with God. He did so as perfect man because He was also fully human. His substitutionary spiritual death on the cross became the basis of our salvation and sealed Satan's doom (Heb. 2:14–15).

When you understand what Christ has done—that He was judged as a substitute for you so you might have eternal life with

---

73. Strategic Victory of the Cross. Phase One: the death, burial, resurrection, ascension, and session of Jesus Christ as the victor in the angelic conflict. Phase Two: the Second Advent, the overthrow of Satan, and crowning of the King. The believer is identified with the strategic victory of Phase One through his union with Christ at the point of salvation; the Church is identified with the second stage of the strategic victory by her return with Christ in resurrection bodies. The tactical victory in the angelic conflict is the normal function of the royal priesthood in the Christian life.

God—and decide to receive His gift of salvation, you have fulfilled the requirement to believe in Him. Faith alone in Christ alone is salvation.

> Believe in the Lord Jesus Christ, and you shall be saved.
> (Acts 16:31*a*)

The faith you express by believing in Christ does not reflect any credit upon you. Believing, as an act in itself, does not make you good enough to merit God's approval. The object of faith, Jesus Christ, has all the merit. The work of Christ on the cross, not your faith, makes your salvation possible. But nevertheless, you are saved the moment you believe in Christ.

Once Jesus Christ accomplished His objective and was seated at the right hand of God, the believers' acceptance in God's presence was assured, as also our position as members of the Royal Family of God (all races and nations, Gal. 3:28), and our function as a Kingdom of Priests. The Church Age had begun. Satan can do nothing about that, nor can he stop the formation of the Body of Christ. Individual human beings with free volition will continue to become believers in Jesus Christ.

Satan continues to make life challenging for the Royal Family. Occasionally he hinders the effective function of the Church, but he can never stop the course of the Church Age. One option left to him is to vent his fierce rage on the Jews. Satan knows only too well that God has planned a glorious future for Israel. He must thwart that promised future at any cost. He must check the overthrow of his own kingdom by the destruction of as many Jews as possible before the Rapture takes place; then he must exterminate these Jews who are left during the Tribulation. If Satan succeeds, God would find it impossible to keep His promises to Israel, for there would be no Jews to rescue and no Jewish client nation to rule.

With that aim in mind, Satan seeks to terminate any possibility for a second strategic victory for Jesus Christ. The Jews must be removed. This is the biblical explanation of anti-Semitism wherever it is found.

ANTI-SEMITISM IN THE FUTURE

It is highly unrealistic to think that man will eventually set aside his prejudices, particularly toward the Jew. For example, assume that our lawmakers introduce additional legislation that favors and protects the Jew. Would this improve human relations? Far from it! Mandating against real or imagined prejudice only aggravates the undercurrent of resentment. At best, statutory compliance can be hoped for; but tolerance and love can never be legislated.

If a change is to come about in man's attitude toward other human beings, that transformation must come from within. Since man possesses a sinful nature and a penchant for prejudice, the answer to his problems is not human reformation but spiritual regeneration, followed by the changes wrought by Bible doctrine in the soul. As long as Satan is the ruler of this world, he will stir up hostility against the Jewish people. Anti-Semitism will continue to exist overtly or covertly until prejudice erupts into unprecedented violence in the middle of the Tribulation.

THE GREAT TRIBULATION

The sixth verse of Revelation 12 skips over the Church Age and the first three-and-a-half years of the Tribulation and presents a future exodus of the believing remnant in Israel.

> And the woman [represents believing Israel in the last half of the Tribulation] fled into the wilderness [the hills and caves of Edom, Moab, Ammon, and Petra] where she had a place prepared by God, so that there she might be nourished for one thousand two hundred and sixty days [the final three-and-a-half years of the Age of the Jews]. (Rev. 12:6)

What will occasion the flight of these Jews? They will correlate Tribulational events with biblical prophecy and align their decisions and actions to pertinent biblical instructions. To sum up these events in sequence: The Rapture will have taken place, and the one hundred and forty-four thousand Jewish evangelists will have gone forth to reap a great harvest of souls (Rev. 7:4, 9–10) among the Jews, especially in the Middle East.

For once, the Jews will feel secure. They will have signed a treaty with the dictator of the Revived Roman Empire, a Gentile, which they assume will ensure their national safety for the next seven years. For certain monetary considerations and payments in the form of natural resources the pact will stipulate that the armed might of the Revived Roman Empire will rush to the aid of Palestine in the event of enemy attack (Dan. 9:27; cf., 11:38–39).

The Temple will have been rebuilt by then, and the sacrifices and rituals prescribed in the Old Testament reinstituted. The nation will be at ease before their trust is shattered. Halfway through the Tribulation, while the treaty is still in force, the dictator of Palestine will issue a new law: Henceforth all sacrifices in the Temple shall cease! In their place, a statue of the dictator of the Revived Roman Empire will be set up in the Most High Place for mandatory worship (Dan. 9:27; 12:11; cf., Rev. 13:15).

The Jews will be stunned by the incredible news. What secret negotiations between their politicians and religious leaders could have concocted this new policy? Must they relinquish their beliefs and traditions to the exigencies of ecumenism and idolatry?

What the general population fails to realize is the true nature of this future dictator of Palestine. His character sketch, presented in the Bible, shows that behind a mask of religiosity and gentle benevolence lurks an egomaniacal tyrant. He is variously identified as "the false prophet" (Rev. 16:13; 19:20), Dan, the serpent (Gen. 49:16–17), and the willful king (Dan. 11:36–40).

A rarely discussed form of anti-Semitism is prejudice toward Jews by other Jews. Remember that Jesus Christ was a Jew in His humanity; yet most of the opposition He encountered came from Jews (John 10:31; 11:47–53). In an effort to prove their complete assimilation into their immediate surroundings, some Jews take on the anti-Semitic attitude of Gentiles. They may find Jewish orthodoxy obnoxious and resent those Jews who are conspicuous for their long, black caftans, beards, and side locks. On the other hand, orthodox Jewry may shun reformed or atheistic Jews.

In this country, some well-educated European Jews, who have immigrated to the United States and have prospered, regard their less refined, Eastern European counterparts with disdain and often with pity. Captain Dreyfus reportedly preferred gentile company and had little sympathy for his Jewish compatriots. The future dictator of Palestine falls into this category. He himself, a Jew from the tribe of Dan, will seek the destruction of his own nation by selling out to the gentile dictator of the Revived Roman Empire, a willing capitulation to demonism.

Under intense pressure, the population of Israel will have an explicit choice. If they resist this latest chicanery, they face deprivation and death (Rev. 13:15–17). Many Jews will weaken and meekly submit to the mark of the Beast—that future identification card patterned after the Roman soldier's serial number burned on his forehead or the back of his hand for all to see. Since most of these people will be unbelievers, they will readily accept what appears to be an opportunity to remain alive. In reality, however, their capitulation to the ecumenical dictator only guarantees their own misery and ultimate destruction (Rev. 14:11; 16:2).

But do not be too hasty in your condemnation of these desperate people. You never know what you might do until you face a similar situation. Remember that Peter, a believer in the Lord Jesus Christ, succumbed to cowardice when his loyalty to Jesus was tested. At that time, he denied the Lord to save his life (Matt. 26:69–74), but this disloyalty led only to terrible self-reproach and bitter tears (Matt. 26:75). Your alternative to betrayal is preparation for disaster by learning and applying God's Word, leaving the results in the hands of the Lord (Ex. 14:13; 1 Sam. 17:47).

Jewish believers in the Tribulation who are knowledgeable in doctrine will heed the Lord's warning.

> Therefore when you see the Abomination of Desolation [the statue of the Roman dictator] which was spoken of through Daniel the prophet [Dan. 9:27], standing in the holy place (let the reader understand), then let those who are in Judea flee to the mountains. (Matt. 24: 15–16; cf., Dan. 11:41; Rev. 12:6)

> For then there will be a great tribulation [disaster], such as has not occurred since the beginning of the world until now, nor ever shall. And unless those days [the

Tribulation] had been cut short, no life would have been saved [delivered]; but for the sake of the elect [believers] those days shall be cut short. (Matt. 24:21–22)

Prophecy, as in Matthew, often has a near and a far fulfillment. In the context of A.D. 70 the Jews are warned to flee from the siege of Jerusalem and the desecration of the Temple by the Roman legions of Titus. The same warning will extend with greater urgency to flee from the armies of the Beast in the days of the Great Tribulation. When the trap is sprung the Jews must take immediate action to survive.

Let him who is on the housetop [roof garden] not go down to get the things out that are in his house [to pack]; and let him who is in the field [at work] not turn back to get his cloak. But woe to those who are with child and to those who nurse babes in those days! But pray that your flight may not be in the winter, or on a Sabbath. (Matt. 24:17–20)

How intensely practical are the words of our Lord. The precaution and haste which He indicated will be absolutely necessary. The setting up of the image in the Temple at Jerusalem will signal the greatest wave of anti-Semitism the world has ever seen. This is the alarm signal for those Jews who know and believe God's Word. Forewarned, they will flee to the places specified in Scripture, where they will find safety and divine provision for their survival.

The plight of these Jewish evacuees will be desperate. People who have been spared the horrors of warfare can scarcely comprehend the accompanying hardships and terrors. The tragedy which civilians must face when their country is attacked, invaded, and conquered is devastating.

During World War II, when France fell to the Germans, all roads were crowded with refugees trying to escape the Nazi advance. Most were older people, women, some of whom were pregnant, and small children. These refugees carried what pitiful possessions they had been able to salvage; others had lost all but their lives.

Then came the merciless enemy aircraft strafing as terrified civilians scurried for cover. Those who had stayed behind fared little better. The havoc wrought by direct enemy assault, the slaughter and atrocities committed against defenseless populations is a price which every defeated nation must pay. These gruesome scenes have been oft-repeated in both ancient and modern times. They will reoccur until the Lord returns (Matt. 24:6). The only way to prevent war is for each generation to be so well prepared for combat that no nation will dare to attack (Judges 3:2).

THE SIEGE OF JERUSALEM, A.D. 70. One of the worst disasters ever to affect the Jews in Jerusalem was the siege of A.D. 70. While that calamity was a result of divine discipline rather than an expression of anti-Semitism, the siege serves as an appropriate illustration of that incomparably greater destruction which is yet to come.

Flavius Josephus, the Jewish historian, provides the most detailed eyewitness account to this holocaust. The horrors defy description.[74] The Holy City, Jerusalem, reeled under the onslaught of wave after wave of Roman infantry as battering rams crashed incessantly against the gates.

Inside the walls, the Zealots, whose fanatical hatred of the Romans prompted their every action, held the city in a tyrannical grip. Jews, known for moderate views and pro-Roman sentiments, were ruthlessly executed. Bands of robbers and cutthroats roamed the streets at will, and no one was permitted to leave the city on penalty of death. Clashes between the Zealots and other groups who opposed them were inevitable. One night, as a result of vicious street fighting, the entire food supply of the city was accidently set aflame. Six to seven years' provisions were lost and the city now faced starvation.

At that time of the year, Jerusalem was teaming with hundreds of thousands of Jews arriving in the city for Passover. They found themselves trapped in a veritable hell-hole of hunger and pestilence. The stench of the dead and dying was unbearable to all but

---

74. Josephus, "The Wars of the Jews," Book V, vi-xiii.

loathsome thieves who stripped corpses of their belongings. In utter despair, the Jews ate even the rats in the streets, and in the end many resorted to cannibalism.

The carnage inflicted by the enemy from without and by the enemy from within was horrendous. Thousands fell prey to the avenging sword, as Caesar ordered the slaughter of the aged, the infirm, and all men under arms who were still in opposition to the Romans. Of the survivors, approximately ninety thousand were taken prisoner. The tallest and most handsome young men were reserved for the triumphal procession down the *Via Sacre* in Rome. Those who were under seventeen years of age were sold into slavery, and those over seventeen were sent to the Egyptian salt mines or to the arenas and certain death.

Then, by the command of Titus, the torch was put to the city and to the Temple. The once magnificent and glorious Jerusalem was reduced to ashes, with the exception of three towers which were to stand as sentinels to the great fortification that Roman valor had subdued.

REFUGE FROM THE SIEGE. As will invariably happen in times of catastrophe, there are those who turn to the Lord in faith and escape harm. This was true during the siege of Jerusalem, and will also be true during the last half of the Tribulation. For all who are caught up in the midst of disaster there is this comfort: Grace is designed for hopeless situations. In grace, God took cognizance of every problem His people would ever face and made provision for it.

God prepared the solution for the Jews of the Tribulation long before the need arose. The mountains of Edom in the southern part of Palestine, Moab in the east, and Ammon (which extends partly into the Sinai Peninsula, the Negev country, and into some of the elevations of Transjordania), make an ideal refuge for those who manage to flee. This remote terrain is wild and inaccessible to armored and mechanized forces, and is of little strategic value to the invader.

WARFARE IN HEAVEN. The Revelation 12 narrative of future political events now permits us to look behind the scenes at open

warfare that will break out in heaven. This is a highly significant
episode which sets certain earthly events into motion. Here is the
real reason why the Tribulational believers in Israel are counseled
to hasten to safety.

> And there was war in heaven, Michael and his angels
> waging war with the dragon. And the dragon and his
> angels waged war. (Rev. 12:7)

It may come as a shock that wars are fought in heaven. But
there has been conflict in heaven since Satan opposed God and
marshaled all hostile angels to his side. The conflict will continue
until Satan is put down at the Second Advent of Jesus Christ.

Presently the heavenly warfare can be classified as a cold war.
This combat takes the form of confrontational verbal assaults in
which Satan tries to argue against the fairness of God with regard
to the judgment of the fallen angels. The struggle is also mani-
fested by his constant accusations against believers (Zech. 3:1–2;
Rev. 12:10) and is seen in the relationship of angelic events to
human history—that is, in Satan's strategy for the world he rules.

Satan has complete files on all living believers, be they of Jewish
or Gentile origin. His excellent and efficient demon intelligence
network carefully annotates every observable sin which you and I
commit. These are taken to the court of heaven. While our sins
may be hidden on earth, they are an open scandal in heaven,
where Satan spends a good part of his time accusing us.

No matter how often we may bungle on earth, in heaven the
devil's blasphemies are always ably refuted by our great Defense
Attorney, Jesus Christ the Righteous (1 John 2:1–2). Each time,
the case is dismissed. In fact, our very existence today and that of
the Jews who live on earth, in spite of every satanic attempt to
annihilate them, depends on Him. In the middle of the Tribulation,
however, the cold war will become a hot war and overflow to
planet earth.

The combatants in the heavenly warfare are described as
"Michael and his angels" on the one side and "the dragon and his
angels" on the other. The mention of Michael is of particular
interest. Not only is Michael the highest of all the elect angels,

with the possible exception of the angel Gabriel, but he is also the guardian angel of Israel (Dan. 12:1; Jude 9).

This high-ranking angel under God's command has occasionally intervened in human history. When Michael battled with the devil over the body of Moses (Jude 9) he was under restraint by the Lord, but this open warfare is the moment he has been waiting for since Satan's prehistoric fall. Michael will lead the elect angels in combat against the demonic hordes.

One can only wonder what type of weaponry and strategy will be used by the angelic host. Do the elect angels wield the sword of the Spirit, which is the Word of God, and do the fallen angels fight back with their fiery missiles (Eph. 6:16)? Certainly the stakes are high; yet the angelic battlefields will not be strewn with the mortally wounded nor with the corpses of angels. Immortal spirit-beings are not subject to physical death. Nevertheless, the hostilities will be as real as those fought upon the earth, and in the epilogue there will be victor and vanquished.

The Greek *polemeo*, meaning "to fight," occurs twice in Revelation 12:7. Conditions of general warfare are indicated, with numerous engagements fought in the vast expanses of heaven. The outcome of the combat is described in a news bulletin which is scheduled for release in the middle of the Tribulation. It reads:

> And they [demonic hordes] were not strong enough, and there was no longer a place found for them in heaven. (Rev. 12:8)

This dispatch depicts a decisive victory, which terminates the raging, all-out battle that banishes Satan and his fallen angels forever from heaven.

> And the great dragon was thrown down, the serpent of old who is called the devil and Satan, who deceives the whole world; he was thrown down to the earth, and his angels were thrown down with him. (Rev. 12:9)

The Greek *ballo*, "to throw down," shows the result of the angelic rebellion and further indicates that Satan and his demons will be exiled from heaven and confined to the earth for the second half of the Tribulation. Observe the biblical identification of the arch-fiend and of all he holds dear. He is variously called "the serpent of old . . . the devil . . . Satan, who deceives the whole world." These names comprise a brief resume of Satan's career. The term, "the serpent of old," refers in the third chapter of Genesis to the real instigator of the fall of man. Satan was present in the Garden at the temptation of Eve when he indwelt the body of the serpent to deceive the woman with artful guile.

Furthermore, Satan has been called, and continues to be called—right up to the middle of the Tribulation—"the devil." *Diabolos* is the English word "slanderer," signifying one of the many stratagems the devil employs in the present cold war in heaven.

The title "Satan" is the hellenized form of the Hebrew *shatan* and means "enemy." Since the beginning of the angelic conflict, *Diabolos* has been the chief and central antagonist. As the legitimate and functional ruler of this world, Satan dominates his subjects by enforcing a policy of deceit. This has always been the case—and will continue to be Satan's mode of control, as brought out by the verb *planao*, "to deceive, to lead astray."

How tragic when a nation is governed by deceit. Policies of deception are always employed by untrustworthy and tyrannical rulers. Sennacherib and Hitler manipulated the masses by deceit. Yet even their cruel ruthlessness is insignificant when compared to the diabolical deception by which Satan dominates his domain. The immense tragedy perpetrated on humanity in those final three-and-a-half years of satanic rule unfolds in this biblical forecast.

> Woe to the earth and the sea; because the devil has come down to you, having great wrath, knowing that he has only a short time. (Rev. 12:12*b*)

FINAL PERSECUTION OF THE JEWS

> And when the dragon saw that he was thrown down to the earth, he persecuted the woman [Israel] who gave birth to the male child. (Rev. 12:13)

Even with the inevitability of his defeat, Satan will not capitulate. Since he is denied access to heaven and cannot vent his rage against God Almighty, he can and will concentrate on the destruction of God's people. This is why the last half of the Tribulation is declared to be the worst period in history for the Jews. As satanically inspired persecution is intensified, the number of martyrs increases alarmingly.

However, the devil's apparent victory will soon turn to disaster. The indomitable faith in Messiah of many Jews and the impact of their testimony, motivated by Bible doctrine in their souls, will mean triumph over the evil one (Rev. 12:11).

Only three-and-one-half years remain to complete Satan's scheme—the annihilation of the Jews. But he can only proceed as far as God permits. In adherence to God's purpose it is allotted to some believers to glorify God in death,[75] while others can serve Him better in life. These Jewish survivors are delivered from the clutches of their unseen supernatural enemy. The same principle of life and death holds true for believers in the present dispensation (John 11:4; 21:19; cf., Phil. 1:20–24).

> And the two wings of the great eagle were given to the woman, in order that she might fly into the wilderness to her place, where she was nourished [fed physically and spiritually] for a time [one year] and times [two years] and half a time [a half-year—three-and-one-half years in all], from the presence of the serpent. (Rev. 12:14)

There has been considerable conjecture regarding a correct interpretation of the eagle's wings. Do they signify escape by aircraft? Some suggest an airlift made possible by courtesy of the United States of America. This is not the meaning. America is not mentioned in prophecy. However, from the use of this same term in other passages in Scripture, we can conclude that the wings of the eagle represent divine protection (Ex. 19:4; Isa. 40:31) from the angelic forces of darkness and their human counterparts.

---

75. *Dying Grace* (1977), 4–6, 11–13.

The escape of so many Jews, who now seem entirely beyond Satan's reach, further infuriates the devil. He must redouble his efforts to enlist the world's armies in the destruction of Israel. Accordingly, his plan goes into operation.

> And the serpent poured water like a river out of his mouth after the woman, so that he might cause her to be swept away with the flood. (Rev. 12:15)

In vibrant imagery, the inspired Word of God describes the invading armies as "water like a river." This military concentration in the Middle East, particularly against Israel in the final campaign, is portrayed as carrying away helpless Jewry in the raging flood's turbulent currents. The identical imagery is utilized in Isaiah 8:7–8, where the king of Assyria is named as the invader of Judah. In the Revelation passage the future King of the North is in view (Dan. 11:40).

The sequence of events, delineated in Revelation 12:16–17, occurs in the reverse order; the war on the Jews (verse 17) precedes the deliverance of that nation (verse 16).

> And the dragon was enraged with the woman, and went off to make war with the rest of her offspring, who keep the commandments of God and hold to the testimony of Jesus. (Rev. 12:17)

Orgizo, "enraged," reveals Satan's attitude toward the Jews. This Greek word depicts irrational, emotional anger, which is a facet of anti-Semitism wherever it is found. The fury of Satan is cumulative antagonism against Israel from the time of Abraham to the end of the Tribulation. This is the background to the war that ends all wars—the Armageddon campaign. Though not mentioned in this passage, the campaign occurs chronologically between the events of Revelation 12:16 and 17.

JERUSALEM AS SATAN'S TRAP

The devil frequently motivates and organizes the movements of militant forces in history. However, the Lord Jesus Christ maintains control over the affairs of mankind. As the omnipotent Creator and sovereign God of the universe, He alone has the final word and ability to overrule or to counter every satanic move. Even though the devil will be responsible for gathering millions of hostile armed men into the Middle East for the last great war, the Lord permits them to converge on their objective (Joel 3:2; cf., Rev. 16:14). He will use Jerusalem as a trap for Satan.

SATAN LURED TO JERUSALEM. Jerusalem has often been and will continue to be a magnet for crisis among the great cities of the world. As the future capital of Israel in the Tribulation, the city will become the center for evangelism, which is reason enough to attract Satan's undivided attention. Following the highly effective ministry of the one hundred forty-four thousand Jewish evangelists in the first half of the Tribulation, Moses and Elijah will return from the dead to herald the Second Advent of Jesus Christ (Rev. 11:3–12; cf., Mal. 4:4–5).

During the period of their return, martyrdom, and subsequent supernatural resuscitation, Moses and Elijah will be given extensive coverage by the news media of their day. The repercussions will be phenomenal (Rev. 11:11–13). For centuries people have been puzzled by and skeptical of the prediction in Scripture that the world's population will be spectators of these unusual happenings in Jerusalem. With the technological advances of television, universal viewing of world events has become a reality that has vindicated God's Word.

There will be further evangelism of the world by supernatural means: An angel will proclaim the everlasting Gospel to every nation on earth (Rev. 14:6–7). Many will respond by believing in Jesus Christ. Concentrated in Jerusalem will be the largest number of born-again Jews in one locale since the time of the Exodus.

While the nations of the world seek to control Jerusalem for its wealth and strategic importance, Satan is also drawn irresistibly to this immense gathering of believing and unbelieving Jews. How easy for Satan to obliterate them. All he must do is maneuver the troops of the major powers into place. Between them the annihilation of the Jews would be only a matter of time. But, Jerusalem represents a trap for Satan, and the Jews are the bait. The master deceiver is being deceived.

PRELUDE TO ARMAGEDDON. By the permissive will of God three of the Satan-inspired, demon-energized combatants will concentrate their forces on Tribulational Israel (Rev. 16:13–14). The opening attack will come from the King of the South, quite possibly Egypt and other Arab nations, and from the King of the North who currently corresponds to the Soviet Union.

The assault of these two allies will be directed initially against the dictator of Palestine (Dan. 11:36–40*a*). Very quickly, however, these kings perceive the real threat to be one another. Yet the King of the South is no match for the King of the North, whose rapid mechanized advance supported by superior naval forces will engulf the entire Middle East (Dan. 11:40*b*).

Jerusalem will be temporarily bypassed as the King of the North pushes his attack into Egypt, but the rest of Israel will ultimately be overrun. Jewish freedom fighters will valiantly defend the beleaguered city. All the Jews—with the exception of those who have hidden in the hill country—will experience a reign of terror (Dan. 11:41–45; Zech. 14:2).

The attacks of the Kings of the North and South will provoke a counterattack from the King of the West (the Revived Roman Empire). With control of Africa at stake, he cannot allow the northern claim to the Middle East to go unchallenged (Dan. 11:42–43). He attacks by sea, and soon fierce naval battles rage in the Mediterranean. The fleet of the King of the North suffers irreparable losses that will sever the sea supply lines to his ground forces in northeast Africa (Dan. 11:44).

To exacerbate the combat, other contenders arrive from the east to join the powers already locked in a death struggle. The Bible refers to them as the "Kings from the East," literally kings of "the rising of the sun" (Rev. 16:12). These are Asian peoples, and their entrance into this theater of war is permitted by the Lord, not by the devil. He who controls history will dispatch one of His administrative angels to dry up the River Euphrates (Rev. 16:12). No sooner is this accomplished than seemingly endless human waves of Asiatics, greedy for spoil, will pour across the dry river bed.

The King of the North is utterly frustrated by the alarming news of this influx of Asiatic powers into the Middle East threatening his land supply lines and severing his sea lane logistics. In uncontrollable wrath he turns against the only people who cannot give him any real opposition—the hapless, defenseless Jews. Then follows the most intensive onslaught of anti-Semitism ever to occur in history. This is not exaggerated prediction but biblical prophecy. The narrative is recorded in these words:

> But rumors from the East and from the North will disturb him [the King of the North], and he will go forth with great wrath to destroy and annihilate many [Jews]. And he will pitch the tents of his royal pavilion between the seas and the beautiful Holy Mountain [Zion]; yet he will come to his end, and no one will help him. (Dan. 11:44–45)

The Soviet Union, which today would represent the King of the North, is well-known for its pogroms and abominable treatment of Jews. With the recent decline of economic and political fortunes, Soviet anti-Semitic attitudes have intensified.[76] If such blatant oppression occurs today, imagine what could happen once Soviet hopes of world domination evaporate. When the war turns against him, the King of the North will launch an offensive to complete what the King of the West and the dictator of Palestine began with the "abomination of desolation"—the annihilation of the Jews. Yet he will be no more successful than any of the others who have raised a hand against them.

WHY ARMAGEDDON? The question arises: Why does the Lord permit such dreadful carnage to afflict the people whom He has chosen and the Land which He has promised them? The answer entails several factors.

1. There is the unseen warfare of the ages. The angelic conflict must run its course; this fight to the finish is Satan's continuing challenge to eliminate the Jews.

2. Intimately related to that conflict, human evil is expressed in personal and national anti-Semitism. God allows negative human

---

76. "Survey in Moscow Sees a High Level of Anti-Jewish Feeling," *New York Times*, 30 March 1990, A6.

volition to function only to a certain point. Ultimately the assault is cut short because of God's promise of protection for the Jews delineated in Genesis 12:3.

3. There is the Jew and his attitude toward God. God offers the Jews, as well as all peoples, a relationship with Him through believing in Jesus Christ, the Messiah (Isa. 52:13—53:12; 1 Pet. 2:24–25; cf., John 3:16–18). As long as the Jews obey God's Word, they are the recipients of tremendous blessings. However, when they bask in disobedience and unbelief, they reap what they sow—divine discipline. When the Jews reject a relationship with *Yahweh* and fail to follow His divine mandates, they incur His wrath (Deut. 28; Prov. 3:12; Ezek. 2). Divine discipline is always commensurate with the offense: The punishment fits the crime (Ps. 7:15–16).

Israel's national discipline began in the first century and will continue until after the Second Advent, when Jesus Christ personally regathers His own people and restores them as believers to the Land. This discipline is the direct result of Israel's rejection of Jesus Christ as their Messiah (Matt. 23:37–39) and their failure to be witnesses for God.

Under divine discipline God explicitly reserves the right to handle all matters concerning the Jews. He needs no help from anyone. Although God condemns anti-Semitism, He allows anti-Semitism to exist in order to accomplish His own purposes. By permitting the anti-Semites into the Land during the Armageddon campaign, God seals their final destruction. When God baits the trap, it snaps shut—not on the bait, but on all who attempt to devour the Jews.

JERUSALEM AS SATAN'S DOOM

In yet another passage, that same trap—Jerusalem—is called a "cup that causes reeling" and a "heavy stone."

Behold, I [God] am going to make Jerusalem a cup that causes reeling to all the peoples around [the four major powers in the Tribulation]; and when the siege is against Jerusalem, it will also be against Judah [the future nation of Israel]. And it will come about in that day [the end of the Tribulation] that I will make Jerusalem a heavy stone for all the peoples; all who lift it will be severely injured. And all the nations of the earth will be gathered against it. (Zech. 12:2–3)

The first illustration portrays Jerusalem as a goblet which God has filled to the brim with believing Jews—a potent drink that will choke all who try to drain its contents by harming the Jews. They shall reel and stagger from drunkenness, which is analogous to the results of divine judgment. "All the peoples" refers to the anti-Semitic nations who contribute armies for the last great siege of Jerusalem.

The second analogy describes Jerusalem as a stone that should not be lifted because of its extreme weight. The "weight" is the promise of God concerning Israel's future. Severe injury results when any nation attempts to interfere with the fulfillment of that promise. Yet anti-Semitic nations will still gather against Israel.

Today, no one has permanently resolved the complexities of the Middle East or the continuing conflict between Arabs and Jews. Neither can anyone explain the enigma of the indestructibility of the Jew apart from the biblical interpretation.

As history unfolds, the situation will become ever more complicated. The biblical prognosis that enmity constantly would exist between half-brothers Ishmael and Isaac and their progeny (Gen. 16:11–12) has been verified over the centuries. The Arabs rarely get along with each other (Abraham sired additional Arab tribes, Gen. 25:2, 6), to say nothing of their hatred for the Jews.

In that future day as civilization advances to the close of the Tribulation, the Bible declares that all peace attempts will ultimately fail. How, then, can those uninitiated to this present Arab-Israeli conflict hope to impose a lasting settlement on the warring factions? Only the personal return of Jesus Christ will put a permanent end to the strife.

Certainly no one is more vitally concerned than Satan to usher in his own peace accord. What an embarrassment to be ruler of this world and to be unable to solve a perpetual dilemma in one's own domain! Satan will attempt a new "final solution" to the Jewish problem in the Jerusalem of the Tribulation. His solution, like that of Hitler, demands the extermination of the Jews, as Satan strives to attain his long-desired victory over Jesus Christ.

Against overwhelming odds, Jewish freedom fighters of the Tribulation will courageously defend the besieged city. Sustained by God's truth in their souls, they will refuse to surrender. They will be willing to die, if necessary, but their martyrdom will exact a heavy price on the enemy (Zech. 12:6).

On the night before the final assault on Jerusalem, millions of the enemy will be poised to strike the fatal blow. Then the trap snaps shut: Supernatural, impregnable darkness will descend on the invaders. The enemy will be immobilized by panic. But that same universal darkness, which terrorizes the foe, will afford protection to the believing remnant.

The darkness will linger for a day; then with startling suddenness the Lord will appear in dazzling light. This is called the day of reckoning (Joel 3:15–16; cf., Joel 2:11). The King of Kings will go forth to fight for His people as He once fought for them in the day of battle at the time of the Exodus (Zech. 14:3; cf., Ex. 14:13–14). The promised Deliverer will come; God keeps His Word.

JUDGMENT OF THE LAST ANTI-SEMITES

Jesus Christ will not permit the anti-Semitism raging at His second coming to contaminate His millennial kingdom. With devastating judgment He destroys the last satanic attack on the Jews. When the glory of Messiah breaks through the darkness, all eyes will be riveted on the blazing light in the clouds (Rev. 1:7). Too late, then, to hide from the recompense (Rev. 6:15–17)! Too late to play the sycophant and assert, "But some of my best friends were Jews!" God has all the facts; He will judge righteously.

Two major personalities that survive the Second Advent will be the dictator of the Revived Roman Empire and the dictator of Palestine. Frantically, they rally their decimated armies for one last defense against the Lord (Rev. 19:19). The armies will meet the very fate they hoped to inflict upon the Jews—total annihilation. Doom awaits the two tyrants.

> And the beast [dictator of the Revived Roman Empire] was seized, and with him the false prophet [dictator of Palestine] . . . these two were thrown alive into the lake of fire which burns with brimstone. (Rev. 19:20)

There they will be joined at a future time by their ally, his majesty the devil (Rev. 20:10).

Both Old and New Testaments portray the judgment of the last anti-Semites as the final vintage of grapes long overripe. Jesus Christ is the Royal Vintager whose golden sickle reaps the harvest of anti-Semites into a winepress in the suburbs of Jerusalem (Isa. 63:1–6; Rev. 14:14–16, 20; 19:15). Isaiah depicts his Messiah clothed in blood-spattered white robes, and John tells how plentiful the deadly harvest will be. As Jesus Christ executes judgment on the enemies of the Jews, their blood is said to flow as high as the horses' bridles for a distance of two hundred miles (Rev. 14:20). It will take seven months to bury the dead (Ezek. 39:14).

In addition to the slaughter of Israel's enemies on the battlefield (Ezek. 38—39), anti-Semitism will be judged throughout the world. The text of Zechariah 14:12–15 graphically pictures how God will deal with the last anti-Semites.

> Now this will be the plague with which the Lord will strike all the peoples who have gone to war against Jerusalem; their flesh will rot while they stand on their feet, and their eyes will rot in their sockets, and their tongue will rot in their mouth. (Zech. 14:12)

This worldwide plague against anti-Semitism does not strike down its victims indiscriminately. The destruction is highly selective and afflicts only those who are already infected by the deadly virus of anti-Semitism in the Tribulation. Medical history has never recorded such a plague. Within moments the diseased victims begin to decompose while they are still living.

Imagine the horror of those who will watch their loved ones and their friends literally rot away. Flesh, which only seconds before was glowing with life and vitality, suddenly decays. Eyes shrivel away in their sockets; and tongues, which uttered curses and blasphemies against the Jews, disintegrate. Only skeletons remain, and they too collapse and crumble away into dust.

> And it will come about in that day that a great panic from the Lord will fall on them; and they will seize one another's hand, and the hand of one will be lifted against the hand of another. (Zech. 14:13)

Panic induced by God turns the tide in favor of His chosen people. As recorded in the Old Testament, God used this type of psychological warfare on Israel's enemies in the day of Moses when the Jews approached the borders of the Promised Land (Deut. 2:25). Panic was employed when Gideon battled the Midianites (Judges 7:19–22), when Jonathan and his adjutant penetrated the camp of the Philistines (1 Sam. 14:1, 6–7), and when the Ammonite invaders were routed (2 Chron. 20:23). Panic will once again immobilize the world's military might immediately before the Second Advent (Zech. 12:4). The horrors of this final panic are unprecedented, the ultimate judgment for anti-Semitism at the end of the Tribulation.

God's punishment always fits the crime. Appropriately the same vicious, irrational hysteria which characterizes anti-Jewish sentiments and movements shall finally manifest itself in mindless, psychotic panic.

> For they sow the wind, and they reap the whirlwind.
> (Hosea 8:7a)

Blinded by hatred, anti-Semites become mentally deranged (Zech. 12:4) and suddenly collapse.

Anti-Semites will accuse their fellow anti-Semites of being Jews. Consequently, the hand which in reality was raised against the Jews now bludgeons a friend. Mass murders will result from this madness. Fittingly, those whose obsession is to exterminate Jewry from the face of the earth will themselves be removed in judgment.

So completely will God scour the world of anti-Semitism that no living creature associated with the armies surrounding Jerusalem will survive. Adam's Fall and subsequent curse affected all lower creation (Rom. 8:19–22). Man's sinfulness brought destruction upon animal life during the Flood (Gen. 7:23). Likewise, anti-Semitism in the Tribulation will adversely affect the animal kingdom.

> So also like this plague, will be the plague of the horse,
> the mule, the camel, the donkey, and of all the cattle
> that will be in those camps [of the anti-Semites]. (Zech.
> 14:15)

While plague devastates the ranks of their adversaries, Jewish soldiers will contribute to the defeat. Now will come their turn to "take the spoil of those who despoiled them" (Ezek. 39:10); now they receive repayment by going through the camps of the hostile armies to collect the wealth of the heathen (Zech. 14:14).

From that moment, when Christ establishes His millennial reign, the fortunes of the Jews will change (Rom. 11:26). As believers who are restored to the Land, they will be the most admired, the most sought-after and respected people in the world (Zech. 8:23). Never again will anti-Semitism erupt; never again will the Land be cursed (Zech. 14:11). Messiah Himself will insure the lasting peace.

6

The Unique Jew

THREE KINDS OF JEWS

IN VIEW OF THE TERRIBLE PERSECUTION which the Jews have suffered in the past and the horror which awaits them in the future, is it incongruous to say that there is an advantage to being a Jew? The third chapter of Romans opens with that very question: in verse 1, "Then, what advantage has the Jew?" and answers the query in verse 2, "Great in every respect!" Before we examine those advantages, however, we must clarify certain biblical terminology.

The Bible uses three designations for God's chosen people. These are technical references which must be properly understood. The terms are: "Hebrew," "Israel," and "Jew." The appellation "Hebrew" was first used of Abraham, whom God had called to be the founder of the Jewish race. After Abraham left Ur of the Chaldees and until he became a citizen of Salem (Gen. 14:17–20), he was a man without a country. He was known as "Abram, the Hebrew" (Gen. 14:13). This means "Abram, the one who crossed the river." That meaning is confirmed by Joshua 24:2–3, which states that the Jewish Patriarchs once "lived beyond the River," the River Euphrates.

The title "Israel," or "prince of God," Jacob's God-given name, was passed down to his progeny. This group of Jews was called the "Children of Israel." Later records designate them as the "Israelites" or "Israel." Biblically, the designation applies to all the tribes, which historically first included the twelve tribes, then, later, the half-tribes of Ephraim and Manasseh—Joseph's descendants. After the defection of the ten northern tribes during the reign of Rehoboam, Israel is referred to as the Northern Kingdom.

The word "Jew" came into use after the Babylonian captivity and indicated members of the tribe of Judah. But today who is a Jew, and who is not? After a stormy debate, the *Knesset*, Israel's parliament, ruled in 1970 that anyone born of a Jewish mother is considered a Jew. Why the mother and not the father? The answer is that although the father cannot always be traced, the mother is generally known.

A Jew can be defined in terms of race, religion, or regeneration. The Word states unequivocally:

> For they are not all Israel, who are descended from Israel: neither are they all children [of God; cf., verse 9] because they are Abraham's [physical] descendants, but: "Through Isaac your descendants will be named." (Rom. 9:6*b*–7)

This passage distinguishes between racial Israel, those who are Jews by birth; religious Israel, those who are Jews by religious tradition; and regenerate Israel, those Jews who have believed in Christ and are members of the Royal Family of God. These same three distinctions apply to the term "Jew" and "Hebrew."

RACIAL ISRAEL

Israel is unique among the races in that its origin is supernatural. When Abraham was no longer capable of procreation and Sarah was beyond the age of childbearing (Gen. 17:17; 18:11–14;

cf., Rom. 4:16–22), God intervened to make the impossible possible (Gen. 18:14). Consequently, through divine rejuvenation of Abraham's and Sarah's ability to propagate, the Jewish race came into existence. Now if God brought about a miracle to usher in the Jewish people, why should anyone, particularly the Jews, reject the miraculous conception and birth of the Savior, who was in His humanity a racial Jew?

The Bible declares any descendant of Abraham who possesses the genes of Isaac, Jacob, or any of the patriarchs to be a racial Jew (Gen. 48:16). He need not be a full-blooded Jew in order to be Jewish. Racial purity is a myth.

Consider the fact that the first Jew was a gentile Chaldean and the early Israelites usually chose their wives within the family (Gen. 24:4; 28:2). Although the Mosaic Law later imposed marriage restrictions upon the Israelites (Deut. 7:3–4; 23:3, 7–8), interracial marriages were not unusual. For example, Joseph's wife was an Egyptian, the daughter of a gentile high priest in Pharaoh's court (Gen. 41:45). Their two sons, Ephraim and Manasseh, were half-Jew and half-Gentile. But they were included among the Israelites and not among the Egyptians (Gen. 48:15–16), causing the original twelve tribes to expand into thirteen tribes (Gen. 48:20).

What qualified Ephraim and Manasseh for acceptance into the Jewish tribal system? Certainly, they had no Jewish mother. Was it deference for Joseph's exalted position? Was it because Joseph had received the double portion of the family inheritance (Gen. 48:22)? No! The basis of their recognition as Jews was twofold: personal relationship to the God of Abraham, Isaac, and Jacob—a spiritual factor, which will be discussed under the category of the regenerate Jew—and secondly, they possessed the genes of Israel; Jewish blood coursed through their veins.

One of the most revered Jews of all time is Moses. A true descendant of the tribe of Levi (Ex. 2:1), Moses married outside the Jewish tribal system. His first wife was a Midianite (Ex. 2:15–21); his second, an Ethiopian (Num. 12:1). Both were Gentiles.

Even in the Davidic line we find intermarriages between Jews and Gentiles. Absalom's mother was an Aramean princess (2 Sam. 3:3); and Solomon's queen, the daughter of Egypt's pharaoh. In fact, most of Solomon's concubines and harem beauties were strangers to the commonwealth of Israel.

In the genealogy of our Lord appear the names of two outstanding gentile women: Rahab, a Canaanite, and Ruth, a Moabite (Matt. 1:5). While records have been lost in the process of Israel's captivity in Babylon and during the dispersion of A.D. 70, the Jews have done a splendid job of tracing their lineage over the centuries. This makes relatively easy a verification of ancestral background to determine whether or not a person is a racial Jew.

RELIGIOUS ISRAEL

Contrary to popular opinion, religion is *not* synonymous with faith in Christ, relationship with the Lord, or devotion to God. As an ingenious counterfeit of the truth, religion is one of the devil's trump cards. Religion emphasizes what man does to earn the approbation of God, as opposed to what God in grace does for man.

When God's grace is removed, the Gospel is obscured (2 Cor. 4:4). Victims of religion are either lulled into complacency concerning their eternal future or their hope for an eternal future is used to enslave them in the legalistic rituals and traditions of man (Mark 7:8; Col. 2:8). The Gospel frees man to serve the living God (John 8:32).

The Bible condemns religion (Jer. 8:8–12; Matt. 23), and rightly so. In the name of religion and alleged Christianity horrible crimes have been committed. When Jews erroneously identify the cross with anti-Jewish persecution, they develop hostility to the declaration of the Gospel, and remain confused about the person and work of Jesus Christ. They reject an intimate, personal relationship with God and choose religion instead.

The religion of the Jews is called Judaism. Modern Judaism evolved from the tenets of the Pharisees and the Sadducees of Jesus' day. Basically, Judaism embraces three divergent views: orthodoxy, conservatism, and reform, with variations among these persuasions.

In practice, the orthodox Jew adheres strictly to the *Torah* and the rabbinical interpretation. The conservative Jew observes the traditional rituals of Judaism but allows for a more liberal interpretation of the religious fundamentals and of the Jewish way of life. Conservative Judaism is, in fact, a compromise between Orthodox and Reform Judaism.

Reform Judaism is both modernized and secularized. As the least stringently demanding, Reform Judaism is the most remote from the traditional definition of Jewry. Between these three views of Judaism is one common bond—loyalty to and interest in the State of Israel.

Although Judaism generally represents the religious Jew, a Jew may or may not be religious. The *Knesset* definition of a Jew states that Jewishness may be a matter of birth *or* a matter of belief. One need not be an ethnic Jew in order to be a religious Jew; one can be a proselyte (Matt. 23:15; Acts 2:10), or one can be both—racial and religious.

REGENERATE ISRAEL

The biblical concept of the true Jew combines racial and spiritual factors. Regarding the racial Jew, the Scriptures declare:

> For he is not a Jew who is one outwardly; neither is circumcision that which is outward in the flesh. (Rom. 2:28)

This statement indicates that overt characteristics are not necessarily proof of Jewishness. The spiritual rebirth mandated, for example, to the Pharisee Nicodemus in John 3:1–18 is a necessity for inclusion.[77]

The ritual of circumcision, which God mandated to Abraham and his male progeny as a sign of the Abrahamic Covenant, had profound spiritual significance. The procedure represented the beginning of the new race founded in the faith expressed by Abraham (Gen. 15:4–6). By circumcision the Jew relates to his unique racial and spiritual heritage. But circumcision was also commanded of all male members of Abraham's household (Gen. 17:9–14) as a principle of blessing by association.

---

77. The only method of spiritual rebirth is declared in John 3:16.

Circumcision is not confined to the Jewish people, but is widely practiced as a sanitary measure, and in some areas of the world used as a rite of initiation. But ritual without reality is meaningless. Therefore, this passage is specific in defining the true Jew as one who is a Jew inwardly—that is, one who is circumcised "of the heart" (Rom. 2:29), after the pattern of Abraham's salvation (Rom. 4:3–5).

"Regenerate Israelite" is the technical designation of a Jew who has believed in the Lord Jesus Christ as He was revealed in the Old Testament. The Jew who accepts Christ as his Savior in the Church Age is unique. In the body of Christ race is no longer an issue. The Jew is entered into union with Christ and becomes a member of the Royal Family of God (Gal. 3:28–29; Col. 3:11; 1 Pet. 2:9).[78] The same spiritual transformation applies to the Gentile; he ceases to be a Gentile and, like the Jew, merges into the Church. Both become one in Christ.

The Apostle Paul was a true Jew in every respect. He referred to himself as a "Hebrew of the Hebrews." A racial Jew, he was descended from the tribe of Benjamin. According to the Mosaic Law, he had been circumcised on the eighth day after his birth. Furthermore, before he was saved, Paul belonged to a religious sect known as the Pharisees and considered himself above reproach in the observance of the Law (Phil. 3:5–6).

In his misguided zeal, he relentlessly persecuted the early Church (Phil. 3:6). Then his own conversion (rebirth or regeneration) occurred (Acts 9:1–6). Although God appointed Paul an Apostle to the Gentiles, Paul deeply desired the salvation of his Jewish compatriots. He expressed his concern in the ninth chapter of his Epistle to the Romans.

> That I have great sorrow and unceasing grief in my heart. For I could wish that I myself were accursed [under a curse] separated from Christ for the sake of my brethren, my kinsmen according to the flesh [racial Jews], who are Israelites, to whom belongs the adoption as sons [God's representatives in the Old Testament],

---

78. *Christian Integrity*, 9–12.

and the glory [personal presence of God], and the covenants, and the giving of the Law [Mosaic Law], and the temple service and the promises, whose are the fathers [Patriarchs], and from whom is the Christ according to the flesh, who is over all, God blessed forever. Amen. But it is not as though the word of God has failed. For they are not all Israel [born-again Israel, the true Jew] who are descended from Israel [racial Israel]. (Rom. 9:2–6)

Once saved, Paul was deeply solicitous for the salvation of his countrymen. Never before had he realized that to be a Jew by virtue of race or religion did not automatically guarantee a favored status in time and eternity. So Paul set out to explain that the Jewish race must be based upon regeneration, which was the original requirement for Abraham, the first Jew, and that the regenerate Jew is the only true Jew in God's sight.

Skillfully, he presented his case. Before Abraham became a Jew, he was already born again (Gen. 15:6; cf., Rom. 4:3). Because Abraham had believed in the promised Messiah, God made him the founder of the Jewish race. Hence, the racial aspect is irrelevant without the spiritual aspect—personal faith in Jesus Christ. The Scripture says, "Whoever believes in Him should not perish, but have eternal life" (John 3:16b). "Whoever" refers to the Gentiles as well as to the Jews: God's offer of salvation extends to every member of the human race.

To prove his point that God differentiates between racial and regenerate Israel, Paul traced the two lineages which sprang from one man—Abraham. Of Abraham's first two sons, one was a Gentile, the other a Jew. Both had the genes of Abraham, yet there was a remarkable contrast between them.

What accounted for the difference? Was it that one was born of Abraham's legal wife and the other of his mistress? No! What differentiated between Abraham's two sons was that one of them was "born again" (John 3:3) while the other was not. Ishmael, the unbelieving Gentile, was blessed for Abraham's sake and became the progenitor of one-third of the Arab people. He is representative of Abraham's "children of the flesh" (Rom. 9:8; cf., Rom. 9:7;

Gen. 16:1–4). Isaac, the regenerate Jew, perpetuated the race in fulfillment of God's promise (Rom. 9:8; cf., Rom. 9:7, 9; Gen. 17:18–19).

The same principle is even more dramatically exhibited in the next generation. One Jewish father and one Jewish mother, Isaac and Rebecca, produced the first recorded set of twins (Rom. 9:10). Puzzled by her condition, Rebecca consulted the Lord.

> And the Lord said to her, "Two nations are in your womb, and two peoples [Jews and Gentiles] shall be separated from your body; and one people shall be stronger than the other; and the older [Esau] shall serve the younger [Jacob]." (Gen. 25:23)

Before the twins were even born or had performed any good or evil, God foretold the divergent paths they would choose. Omniscience foresaw that Jacob would express faith and Esau would reject salvation. Therefore God declared, "Jacob I loved, but Esau I hated" (Rom. 9:13). Divine approval is never based on human works (Rom. 9:11; Eph. 2:8–9; Titus 3:5) but on man's response to the grace of God which brings salvation to all mankind (Titus 2:11).

Note the brilliance of Paul's exposition. He chose for his illustration the contrast between the Jews and the Gentiles. The Jews understand and nod in agreement; they identify with Abraham, Isaac, and Jacob. They are proud of their ancestry and prone to disdain the Gentiles.

Then the truth dawns on them—a like contrast exists among themselves: *"They are not all Israel who are descended from Israel"* (Rom. 9:6). Old Testament documentation supports Paul's claim: "Though the number of the sons of Israel [racial Israel] be as the sand of the sea, it is the remnant [only] that will be saved [regenerate Israel]" (Rom. 9:27; cf., Isa. 10:22–23).

The great Apostle laments the tragedy of his people whose zeal for religion has blinded them to the truth (Rom. 11:8, 25). They readily accept the Law, which demonstrates the sinfulness of mankind and his need of a Savior (Rom. 3:20), but they reject the only One who fulfilled the Law perfectly (Matt. 5:17; cf., Rom. 8:3–4) and thereby met God's standards for them. They bypass

God's requirement of perfect righteousness, which can only be attained by faith in Jesus Christ, and attempt to establish their own relative righteousness, a righteousness that is totally unacceptable to God (Rom. 9:31; 10:3; cf., Isa. 64:6).

Grace and legalism are mutually exclusive (Rom. 11:6). God's grace gift of Jesus Christ and the decision to believe in Him divide regenerate Israel from racial and religious Israel. With this in mind, Paul exclaims, "Brethren, my heart's desire and my prayer to God for them [Israel] is for their salvation" (Rom. 10:1).

But Israel's rejection of the Savior is neither total (Rom. 11:1–10), nor is it final (Rom. 11:11–32). Only to the regenerate Jew is Jewishness an advantage.

> Then what advantage has the Jew? Or what is the benefit of circumcision? Great in every respect. First of all, that they were entrusted with the oracles of God [the Old Testament Scriptures]. (Rom. 3:1–2)

The Greek word for "advantage" is *perissos*, which means "over and above." *Perissos* indicates the extraordinary, the remarkable. The exact meaning this passage conveys is one of preeminence. The answer to Paul's rhetorical question deals with Israel's past and defines the advantages of the Jews in the Age of Israel as one of privilege and responsibility.

THE ADVANTAGE OF BEING A JEW

In the short phrase, "Great in every respect" (Rom. 3:2), all of Israel's advantages are brought into focus. These advantages are linked to God's Word. To Israel this meant:

1. *Salvation advantages*: the born-again Jews' temporal and eternal security, which is expressed in the four unconditional covenants;

2. *Dispensational advantages*: custodianship of God's Word in written and verbal form (Rom. 3:2); blessings through obedience to Bible doctrine;

3. *Ritual advantages*: a clear declaration of the person and work of Messiah in shadow form; circumcision of heart, which was symbolized by the rite of circumcision on all Jewish males;

4. *Racial and national advantages*: all blessings accrued through grace and through the inculcation of Bible doctrine; the nation benefited from the presence of regenerate Jews in their midst;

5. *Establishment advantages*: the giving of the Mosaic Law as a charter of human freedom; adherence to the Law ensured spiritual and financial prosperity, and military success for Israel.

ISRAEL'S PAST

From the call of Abraham to the time of the Exodus and from their wanderings in the desert through their turbulent history as a nation, Israel was ever the recipient of God's bountiful grace. None of us—Jew or Gentile—earn or deserve preferential treatment from God; yet it pleased God to make the Jews His own special people.

All divine revelation which has been reduced to writing came to and through Israel. Every writer of the Old Testament Scriptures was a Jew. Furthermore, God made the Jews the beneficiaries of four unconditional covenants. This everlasting treaty, into which God entered with Abraham and with his born-again progeny (Gen. 17:7), consists of four separate paragraphs and guarantees the Jews a future, a purpose, and a title deed to a land of their own. Because the covenants are unconditional in nature, their fulfillment depends solely upon the character of God. The four paragraphs of the unconditional covenants are described below:

Paragraph One: *The Abrahamic Covenant* (Gen. 12:1–3) establishes the Jewish race and the future nation Israel and anathematizes anti-Semitism (Gen. 13:14–17; 15:1–7, 18; 17:1–8).

Paragraph Two: *The Palestinian Covenant* (Gen. 13:14–15) promises the Jews a specified territory in the Middle East and secures the final restoration of Israel in this land after the Second Advent of Jesus Christ (Isa. 11:11–12).

Paragraph Three: *The Davidic Covenant* (2 Sam. 7:8–16; 22:51) perpetuates the Davidic dynasty through the eternal reign of Christ (Luke 1:32; Acts 2:29–30).

Paragraph Four: *The New Covenant* (Jer. 31:31–34) confirms the future of Israel in spite of the administration of the fifth cycle of discipline to both the Northern and Southern Kingdoms, and relates the future of Israel to the First Advent and strategic victory of Christ, which includes the cross, resurrection, ascension, and session.

ISRAEL'S SUPERIORITY

The preeminence of Israel is clearly seen in God's assurance to Abraham that the Jews would live throughout history despite every satanic attempt to destroy them, and that every born again Jew—from Abraham to the Second Advent—would have a phenomenal place in the eternal plan of God.

Such promises were never made to any other race or nation—only to Israel. This means that God has obligated Himself to keep His Word to the Jews. At the time when Abraham left Ur of the Chaldees and entered into the grace covenant with God, the Anglo-Saxon race was still in a barbarous or, at best, a semi-barbarous state. Established on God's selection of Israel as His chosen people, the Jews could have appointed themselves a "superrace." However, by revealing His divine purposes to Israel and using divine discipline when they deviated from His purposes, God saw to it that they did not exalt themselves.

Historically, the superiority of the Jews is demonstrated by the fact that God established them, first as a race, then as a nation. God gave them not only His laws of salvation and spiritual function, His laws of divine establishment and human freedom, but He also ruled personally over the nation as a theocracy for the first four hundred years.

The Jewish race was perpetuated on the foundation of regeneration, and the nation was composed exclusively of believers when the Exodus generation first emerged from slavery in Egypt.[79] The distinction (Eph. 2:17–19) between Israel and her gentile neighbors—and all the nations of the world down through the centuries—is the fact that Israel began as a regenerate theocracy. This divine heritage has propelled the Jews through a long and illustrious history. Though not perfect by any means, the Jews have always had a system of laws and the superior advantage of being "the pupil of God's eye"—His protected and chosen people. No gentile nation can make such a claim.

The cultural superiority of the Jews is also evident. Whereas many of our gentile ancestors still lived in caves and hovels under the most primitive conditions, the ancestors of the Jews had an advanced standard of living. Given to Israel by God, the Mosaic Law insured these standards.

The Jews had hygienic laws commensurate with today's standards. They possessed an equitable system of justice and a superior moral code. They practiced soil conservation and rotation of crops. Their excellent dietary laws contributed to the nation's health. They produced inspired artisans, poets, and musicians; extraordinary statesmen and warriors; judges and kings. No matter how cruelly they were persecuted through the centuries, the Jews never suffered disintegration of their cultural or spiritual standards.

As a special people with a unique mission and a lofty purpose in life, the Jews were not only singularly blessed, they were also liable to particularly severe punishment. Their reversionistic failures were punished with the appropriate divine discipline—discipline designed by a loving, gracious heavenly Father to train and correct His children (Prov. 3:12; Heb. 12:6).

---

79. At the first Passover in Egypt, the blood of an unblemished lamb was placed on the two doorposts and on the lintel of the houses (Ex. 12:5–6, 13). The ritual expressed the believing faith of those who would participate in the Exodus, the same faith that Abraham exhibited in Genesis 15:6. The blood of the spotless lamb was a picture of the blood of Christ, which would be shed on the cross, paying the price for their salvation.

ISRAEL'S PRESENT

Israel is currently under divine discipline for:

1. Unbelief or rejection of salvation on the part of racial and religious Jewry;

2. Failure to accomplish the mission which God had entrusted to them as the elect nation.

This discipline began in A.D. 70 when God scattered the Jews to the ends of the earth. Although a handful of Jews have returned to the Land, the majority will remain dispersed until Jesus Christ regathers them at His second coming.

Since 1948 Jewish achievements in Palestine must be recognized as splendid. The current nation of Israel has secured and expanded its borders, winning reprieve and respect through its military prowess. They have created a homeland for displaced and desperate Jewish refugees. The new inhabitants have done a magnificent job in reclaiming this beautiful land from an arid desert.

The Jews have demonstrated to the world that they have never lost their vigor. Most other peoples would have been defeated by the constant political and military pressure. Ferociously repulsing any threat to their sovereignty, the Jews are more realistic about aggression from antagonistic nations than any other free nation. They are prepared to fight to maintain their autonomy and freedom; they are willing to make whatever sacrifices are demanded of them.

Since the interruption of the Jewish Age, the plan of God no longer centers on Israel. The believing Jew loses identity with race and family when united with all Church Age believers into one new creation—the Body of Christ—the technical designation for the Church on earth. While the unregenerate Jew is still protected by the anti-Semitism clause in Genesis 12:3, spiritual benefits to the Jew during the Church Age must come through individual faith in Jesus Christ.

Besides those which have been enumerated, there are countless advantages and blessings that accrue to believers with spiritual growth and maturity through Bible doctrine resident in the soul.[80] Even greater are the privileges all believers will enjoy in time to come. The Israel of the future is no exception.

ISRAEL'S FUTURE

Israel's future was first declared at the founding of the Jewish nation (Ex. 6:2–8). That future began with the acceptance of the Savior (John 3:36; cf., Rom. 9:6–14). Likewise, your future was assured the very moment you believed in the Lord Jesus Christ (John 3:16). Thus, the futures of Israel and Church Age believers depend solely on the gracious character of God.

Israel's future is related to a section of real estate—Palestine. God promised this region to Abraham at a time when it looked as though he were about to lose out on a land deal. Genesis 13 records the background of the quarrel over grazing rights between the "cowboys" of Abraham and Lot. The result was a severance of family ties that freed Abraham to pursue God's plan for his life (Gen. 12:1).

To settle the dispute, Abraham gracefully relinquished to young Lot the first choice of territory that stretched out before them. Abraham was motivated by faith in God's promise; Lot was blinded by human viewpoint and greed. Lot chose and settled in the land of Canaan and the cities of a lush valley, which included Sodom (Gen. 13:10–13). There he hoped to carve out a cattle empire for himself. It is noteworthy that there has never been a "Lotsville" or a nation founded by Lot. Instead, there is a salt and chemical depository—the Dead Sea—in the exact spot that Lot picked.

Abraham, on the other hand, gained blessing from his gracious generosity toward Lot and his dependence on the Lord. As far as his eyes could see in all directions—from the Euphrates to the Jordan, from the Mediterranean to the end of the Negev—God promised this land to him and to his seed forever (Gen. 13:14–15). To this very moment, the Jews have never yet occupied the entire

---

80. *The Divine Outline of History*, 80–135.

area which God promised to Abraham, but they will in the Millennium.

How does the present status of the Land compare to its future? There is no comparison. The Millennium begins only with believers. The desert will vanish and become a veritable Eden (Isa. 35:1–2, 7). Prosperity and health will abound (Isa. 35:5–6). Complete happiness, peace, and contentment will pervade the Land (Isa. 35:10) and violence will be virtually nonexistent (Isa. 60:18). As for the descendants of anti-Semites, they will flock to the Jews with a totally changed attitude. Jerusalem will draw them like a magnet.

> And the sons of those who afflicted you will come bowing to you, and all those who despised you will bow themselves at the soles of your feet; and they will call you the city of the Lord, the Zion of the Holy One of Israel. (Isa. 60:14)

Never again will hostile armies march on Jerusalem. Instead, their offspring will make annual pilgrimages to the Holy City, which will then be the capital of the world. Her gates will be open continually to welcome the faithful.

> Then it will come about that any who are left [believers] of all the nations that went against Jerusalem will go up from year to year to worship the King, the Lord of hosts, and to celebrate the Feast of Booths. (Zech. 14:16)

For "the Holy One of Israel" is enthroned in Zion, the "city of the Lord."

The future of Israel is inseparably connected to the eternal reign of Messiah, Jesus Christ. Where, then, does the Royal Family fit into the picture? Believing Jews and Gentiles of the Church Age will occupy a prominent place in the Millennium. As God's elite, the regenerate "will be priests of God and of Christ, and will reign with Him for a thousand years" (Rev. 20:6).

What a pleasure it will be to watch the regathered survivors of the Tribulation live side by side with the resurrected saints of the Old Testament in perfect environment (Isa. 26—27; Dan. 12:13).

What a privilege to have an active part in the affairs of redeemed Jewry as co-regents with the Shepherd of Israel (Isa. 40:11).

But Israel's future extends far beyond the Millennium into eternity. When the present heavens and earth have been destroyed by divine cataclysmic judgment (2 Pet. 3:7), God will reproduce "a new heaven and a new earth" in pristine beauty and perfection (Rev. 21:1, 5).

Then, Abraham will receive his city, "whose Builder and Maker is God" (Heb. 11:10; cf., Rev. 21:10–27). The Jerusalem and Palestine of the new earth will belong to the Jews, and the rest of the earth will be divided among the saved Gentiles of previous dispensations. The home of the Church is the new heavens, for we are said to be a heavenly people. At the end of the thousand years, God's plan for human history will have run full cycle; the eternal state begins.

We can rejoice in the grace of God and in the knowledge that man's failures do not hinder the plan of God. Israel's past with its sublime glory and subsequent apostasy and decline, the present Israel with its discipline, problems, persecutions, and pressures will be blotted out by the promised grandeur. Israel *has* a future.

7

Applying Biblical Principles to Anti-Semitism

THE CHRISTIAN ATTITUDE TOWARD THE JEW

A BELIEVER INVOLVED IN ANTI-SEMITISM is in direct opposition to the will and plan of God. When we become Christians our background prejudices and preconceived notions carry over into the Christian life. These irrational intolerances have a tendency to cling like barnacles on a ship.

Have we forgotten that not too long ago we as unbelievers

> were at that time separate from Christ, excluded from the commonwealth of Israel, and strangers to the covenants of promise, having no hope and without God in the world. (Eph. 2:12*b*)

Only through the intake and application of God's Word, which includes accepting the biblical view of anti-Semitism, can we progress spiritually to the point of overcoming our prejudices and misjudgments.

As stiff-necked, ex-Gentiles we thank God for grace when we fail, but hypocritically wish God to judge those we may think are obnoxious. We implore the Lord for help and expect divine deliverance; yet we would deny that same grace to others, particularly to the Jews. There is no place for arrogance or self-righteousness in the Christian life. We have no corner on the market where God's grace is concerned. Grace is extended to all.

THE WILD VERSUS THE NATURAL BRANCHES

In his Epistle to the Romans, the Apostle Paul warns Christians against the folly of anti-Semitism. With the advent of the Church Age, these believers had erroneously assumed that God had no further use for the Jews; consequently, neither had they. Paul counters their presumptuous perspective with two questions:

1. "God has not rejected His people, has He?" (Rom. 11:1)

2. "They did not stumble so as to fall, did they?" (Rom. 11:11)

Paul's answer to both questions is *me genoito*, a dogmatic, emphatic *no*! As the strongest negative in the Koine Greek, *me genoito* should be translated "may it never be." Even though Israel is presently under the fifth cycle of discipline, Jews continue to live upon the earth. In every generation some Jews will accept Christ as their Savior and be numbered among the "remnant according to God's gracious choice" (Rom. 11:5).

Concerning the fall of Israel, the discipline is national rather than personal. God never intended that Israel's dispersion should lead to racial destruction. Far from it! God turned cursing into blessing. The administration of divine discipline accomplished what divine blessing had failed to bring about—the salvation of a maximum number of Jews. Enjoying divine blessing in the Land, they had rejected Christ in large numbers. But scattered throughout the earth, suffering under divine discipline, many would respond to the Gospel. Moreover, through the discipline of Israel, blessings accrue to the Gentiles.

Israel's spiritual heritage made the Jews a great nation, and this unique heritage contributed blessings to the rest of the world. Gathered in one country, the Jews became clannish and parochial, refusing to go out as missionaries. Jonah is a classic example of this unfortunate, provincial attitude.

God commissioned Jonah to go to Nineveh and proclaim a gracious warning of impending judgment. So antagonistic was the prophet toward the Assyrians, his nation's enemies, he fled in the opposite direction (Jonah 1:1–3) wishing them destroyed rather than spared. When God overruled and compelled His messenger to obey the divine command, Jonah sulked over the success of his mission (Jonah 3:10; 4:1–3).

With the passing of time, Israel departed from grace and developed a legalistic religiosity. The stronger this legalism became, the more the Gospel and the grace of God were obscured. All these things contributed to the nation's fall.

Repeatedly, God pleaded with His people to return to Him, but the pleas fell on deaf ears. Rejection of the Gospel of salvation had blinded most of Israel (Rom. 11:27). There comes a time when fledglings must leave their nest; the parent bird nudges them to the edge. If the gentle prodding is continually ignored, the birds must be pushed for their own good. And so, God's scattering of the Jewish people from their land became a means of worldwide evangelism.

Accordingly, "their transgressions [their national discipline]" became "riches for the world" (Rom. 11:12), and "their rejection" became "the reconciliation of the world" (Rom. 11:15). Whereas once God had representatives based in only one geographical area, He now had ambassadors in the far regions of the earth. Wherever these Jews went, they took with them the Word of God—their spiritual heritage. By being scattered, they became a blessing to the nations of the world. Thus, the dispersion of Israel is mutually beneficial to both Jews and Gentiles.

The interruption of the Jewish Age and the cessation of the Jewish nation's special duties as custodians and disseminators of the Word of God inaugurated the Church Age and the appointment of believing individuals to assume that sacred trust (Acts 1:8). The twelve apostles, all of whom were Jewish, journeyed throughout the world to spread the Gospel (Matt. 28:19). Although Paul had been designated as an "Apostle of Gentiles" (Rom. 11:13), he considered himself a debtor "to the Jew first, and also to the Greek [Gentile]" (Rom. 1:16b). He declared that he owed "the gospel, for it is the power of God for salvation to every one who believes" (Rom. 1:16a), but first of all to the Jews. Yet the more Gentiles that are saved, the more Jews will be reached through contact with the Gospel.

Although a greater number of Jews will accept Christ as Savior in the Church Age than in the Age of the Jews, the majority of the Royal Family of God will be Gentiles. Paul anticipates the reaction of the Jews toward the blessing of the Gentiles who once were "without Christ . . . excluded from the commonwealth of Israel, and strangers from the covenants of promise . . . but now in Christ . . . have been brought near by the blood of Christ [His expiatory sacrifice on the cross]" (Eph. 2:12–13). Paul hoped that this would stimulate many Jews to follow his example and trust in Jesus Christ (Rom. 11:14).

In no way does the interruption of the Jewish Age give the Gentiles a license to be condescending or to put pressure on the Jews. The Gentile owes his place in the present dispensation strictly to the grace of God. The failure to grasp this significant truth led early Christians to embark on an anti-Semitic course. Therefore, Paul deemed it vitally important to immediately reverse this trend among believers. Using nature as his illustration, the Apostle launched a timely instruction utilizing the olive tree and its branches.

> And if the first piece of dough [Abraham, Isaac, Jacob] be holy [saved], the lump [the rest of Israel] is also; and if the root [Jesus Christ] be holy, the branches [saved Jews in the Church Age] are too. But if some of the branches [unbelieving Jews of all time] were broken off, and you [saved Gentile], being a wild olive, were grafted in among them [believing Jews], and became partaker with them of the rich root of the olive tree [Jesus Christ], do not be arrogant toward the branches [*a warning against anti-Semitism*]; but if you are arrogant,

> remember that it is not you who supports the root [you
> do not hold up Christ], but the root supports you [a
> reference to the believer's eternal security]. (Rom.
> 11:16–18)

This warning from Paul's day must be reiterated and applied
today. As a believer, you must honor the spiritual heritage of the
Jews and *beware of anti-Semitism*, for God will not tolerate
continued disobedience to His command. You who are guilty of
anti-Semitism are guilty of a terrible sin. Your prejudicial mental
attitude and overt conduct are totally antithetical to a member of
the Royal Family of God. Even though you are eternally secure in
Christ, you have brought discredit upon the Lord, and God will
deal with you personally and severely.

Look again at the olive tree and its branches! The olive tree has
long been the symbol of Israel (Hosea 14:5–6). Firmly rooted in
Messiah by faith, the patriarchs founded the Jewish race. The race,
in turn, drew strength from spiritual nourishment, the sapling
grew into a sturdy tree and branched out into a vigorous nation.
As the tree spread, however, it became obvious that some of the
branches did not belong.

These branches depicted racial but unregenerate Israel. Refusing
to draw their life-giving waters from the well of salvation (Isa.
55:1–6), they drank, instead, from the river of religion. They
rejected salvation by grace through faith and chose a system of
works by which they hoped to gain the approbation of God. They
were dead branches and had to be broken off the tree—a picture
of divine judgment.

This pruning of dead branches left gaps in the tree. Although at
one time in Jewish history—at the time of the Exodus—all who left
Egypt were redeemed, Israel did not maintain solid ranks. Thus,
God filled these gaps with believing Gentiles; wild olive branches
were grafted into the good olive tree.

During the administration of the fifth cycle of discipline to Israel,
the olive tree becomes the Church, and Jew and Gentile alike are
"partakers . . . of the rich root [in union with Christ]" (Rom.
11:17). To the believing Gentile of Paul's era, this new position
became the basis for inordinate pride and the premise for a false

deduction: "Branches [unbelieving Jews] were broken off [by God] so that I might be grafted in" (Rom. 11:19).

Note the emphasis on self, the height of conceit—God preferred *me*! Devoid of grace orientation, their blatant arrogance emerges. Can you detect a smug racial superiority, which is so characteristic of anti-Semites? What was the real reason for the removal of the dead wood from the tree?

> Quite right, they were broken off for their unbelief, and you [believing Gentile] stand only by your faith. Do not be conceited, but fear; for if God did not spare the natural branches [unbelieving Jews], neither will He spare you. (Rom. 11:20–21)

The warning is unmistakable; the wild olive branches must never think that they are better than the natural branches: "For all have sinned, and come short of the glory of God" (Rom. 3:23*a*). The Jews were broken off because of their unbelief; the Gentiles were grafted in because they believed in Christ (John 3:36). Standing "only by your faith" indicates that believing Gentiles will always remain in a saved status. They were saved by nonmeritorious faith through the grace of God. Their union with Christ, their oneness with the natural branches, depend on who and what Christ is and always excludes pride. Instead of being anti-Semitic, Christians should be gracious toward the Jew lest they suffer the consequences of divine discipline. Paul's warning, "If God did not spare the natural branches, neither will He spare you" (Rom. 11:21) is pertinent to all anti-Semites.

> Behold then the kindness [love, gentleness, beneficence] and severity [righteousness and justice] of God; to those who fell, severity [toward the broken off branches], but to you God's kindness, if you [saved Gentile] continue in His kindness; otherwise you also will be cut [broken] off. (Rom. 11:22)

Genesis 12:3 remains in force and applies to Jews and Gentiles alike. The fact that you are in the Royal Family forever does not exempt you from divine discipline. Note the conditional clause, "if you continue in His kindness!" God's blessing will continue as long as you continue to grow in grace, which includes avoiding anti-Semitism. But divine love must express itself in divine justice once you stray from the path which God delineated for you in His Word. While you cannot lose your salvation, God's final divine discipline will remove you from this life, if you persist on the disastrous course of anti-Semitism.

How do you avoid anti-Semitism? Through knowledge of Bible doctrine, which is indispensable to the Christian life (Rom. 11:25). Bible doctrine will make improvements in your soul, weeding out the arrogance, prejudice, and intolerance. The writer of Hebrews addresses believers who have drifted from the path of grace:

> But, beloved, we are convinced of better things concerning you, and [even] things that accompany salvation. (Heb. 6:9a)

The principle of continuing in His kindness is the same for Jews and Gentiles. As a result two changes occur: a change of thought pattern and a change of activity. Both are accomplished in the filling of the Spirit through Bible doctrine in the soul. Pride, envy, and hatred are replaced by orientation to doctrine by means of spiritual growth. Doctrine is designed to solve all problems of the Christian's attitude toward the Jew. More than that, doctrine specifies what the proper attitude should be: a desire to evangelize them, respect for their past, and support for their future. Remember that there are all kinds of Jews, even as there are all kinds of Gentiles; we all possess sin natures. To help you regard the Jew in the proper perspective, consider the following guidelines.

GUIDELINES ON EVALUATING THE JEW

1. *Evaluate the Jew as an individual.* Evaluate him *objectively* as you would anyone. Doubtless you have been evaluated many times with regard to your personality, thought pattern, poise, attractiveness, athletic ability, capability in some field, or in any of the many ways in which individuals and their potential are estimated. But you should never evaluate a person on the basis of race or color

of skin. Instead, evaluate them on the basis of their ideas and integrity.

A Jewish unbeliever should be appraised as you would any other unbeliever: as a person without Christ and in need of the Gospel. If his standards line up with the laws of divine establishment, you may approve on that basis. But *never*, under any circumstances, regard yourself as a judge or an instrument of divine discipline to the Jew.

2. *Evaluate the Jew as a Christian.* "Do not judge lest you be judged yourselves" (Matt. 7:1). Jews who have found Jesus Christ as Lord and Savior in this dispensation are as much in union with Christ as are gentile believers—branches in the same tree. They are no longer considered Jews but Christians.

> There is neither Jew nor Greek, there is neither slave
> nor free man, there is neither male nor female; for you
> are all one in Christ Jesus. (Gal. 3:28)

Therefore, you should have the same attitude toward born-again Jews as you have toward any other Christian. That attitude is mandated in Scripture (Rom. 12:16; 1 Thess. 5:12–13) and achieved through spiritual growth (Eph. 4:14–16).

You have no right to criticize a fellow believer. Judgment is God's prerogative. God has all the facts, and only He can fairly evaluate family matters of that nature. This principle does not rule out legitimate evaluation for the purpose of church leadership, secular leadership, or qualified employment, where a reference is required. However, the divine mandate forbids all gossip, maligning, and censure within the Royal Family of God. Just remember that all Christians have the right of privacy and spiritual freedom to live their lives as unto the Lord.

3. *Evaluate Israel as a nation.* This poses something of a problem. What remained of the once-great Jewish nation was scattered throughout the world in A.D. 70, when God allowed Rome to administer the fifth cycle of discipline, beginning the second dispersion. Israel as an elect nation is now set aside until the Second Advent of Jesus Christ. At that future time the nation will

consist of regathered, living, born-again Jews and resurrected Old Testament saints.

Today, America is a host nation for dispersed Jews and should receive these people as we would any other. When they become citizens, they are simply Americans with a different ethnic background, not an uncommon circumstance in the history of the United States. Jews who choose to immigrate to other countries merge and adapt to the culture of their adopted nation.

What of Palestine as a homeland for the Jews? This, as we saw, is God's design for Israel's future. The present gathering of the Jews in Israel is of no prophetic significance; it is *not the regathering* of national Israel forecast in the Scriptures. The Israeli nation which exists today has man's, not God's, stamp of approval. Consequently, the present Jewish state is evaluated on its national and international policies, adherence to law, and the host of other criterion upon which we approve or disapprove the actions of any allied nation. Notably, since Israel's inception in 1948, the United States has maintained close diplomatic and political relations.

Where does the American Jew's allegiance belong? Is he obligated to Israel because he is a Jew, or to America because he is an American? Some Zionists argue that every Jew's loyalty should be directed toward the Jewish homeland. This is not so! Americans owe their allegiance to the flag of the United States. However, if an American Jew wishes to contribute to the support of Israel, he may do so on the same premise as he would any cause he deems worthy; but this should not be an arbitrary demand. An American Jew is in no way obligated to the Jewish nation.

As for the Christian's attitude toward Israel, there is no command in Scripture to reverence that nation as some sacred cow. As with all nations Israel has good and bad policies and must stand or fall on its own merits. Neither malign nor deify Israel, but evaluate her policies as you would any other nation—on the basis of your knowledge of Bible doctrine. Currently Israel is one of the few countries that understands freedom through military victory.[81] Therefore, respect Israel for its patriotic, courageous stand.

---

81. See *Divine Establishment*, 20–30.

4. *Evaluate the Jew as an American.* How do you evaluate an American? You evaluate him by certain fundamental principles: his convictions, his patriotism, his political beliefs, his opinions. Are his norms and standards compatible with those delineated in the Constitution and Bill of Rights? You extend this courtesy to the gentile American and to the Jewish American alike.

5. *Evaluate the Jew using doctrine and common sense.* May God the Holy Spirit help you to make the correct applications of the Bible doctrines outlined in this book. May you have the perceptive ability to wade through the false and see only the true issues in this crucial period of our history as a nation.

From the divine perspective a nation's continued existence depends on several factors: adherence to the divine laws of establishment, dissemination of doctrine, spiritual freedom, evangelism, missionary activity, and an attitude of toleration and support toward the Jews. Your personal attitude is important because nations are composed of individuals. As goes the believer, so goes the nation.

There is only one people whom God has promised to preserve throughout history—the Jews. They may be scattered and persecuted, but they have never been obliterated nor have they lost their racial identity. Jews are blessed above all other peoples of the earth as a constant testimony to the veracity and authenticity of the Word of God—a perpetual reminder of His grace and faithfulness.

Epilogue

THE SPECTER OF MILITANT ANTI-SEMITISM once again casts its lethal shadow over world affairs and the lives of Americans. On 2 August 1990 Iraq invaded Kuwait launching yet another paroxysm of hostilities across that war torn region. Within the month the United States at the request of the Saudis responded to Saddam Hussein's aggression by committing air, naval, and ground forces to defend Saudi Arabia and other imperiled Middle Eastern states. Thus began the largest U.S. military deployment since the Viet Nam War. Over five hundred thousand American troops were poised for combat in Saudi Arabia. Israel supported U.S. actions against Iraq and stood ready to contribute all her military power.

In a counter strategy Hussein took thousands of hostages and declared a holy war against the United States and Israel. With inflammatory accusations he attempted to rally further Arab support by casting U.S. troops as crusading infidels. Hussein then played his trump card of anti-Semitism. By invoking old hatreds and paranoia against Israel, he sought to justify his rape of Kuwait and to neutralize the already precarious alignment of neighboring Arab states with the United States.

Saddam Hussein risked a huge gamble. His incursion into Kuwait was not just an economic maneuver to plunder Kuwaiti wealth and control thirty percent of the world's oil reserves. The more salient motivation was political: Hussein yearned to establish his leadership in the Arab world, to wear the mantle of a modern day Nebuchadnezzar, and to conclusively crush Israel.

Considered arrogant, the rich Kuwaitis were envied and unpopular among their jealous Arab neighbors. Further aggravating Arab resentment Kuwait has been a bastion of cooperation with the West. Hussein surmised that by smashing this tiny country, he would secure his role as an effective and charismatic commander for the radical Arab states. Those states would accept him as the champion for a united Arab front against Israel and the West. Terror engendered by Hussein's reputation for ruthlessness would prevent more moderate Arab nations from organizing opposition to his hegemony.

The Iraqi strongman, startled by the swift American response to his aggression, arrogantly refused to capitulate to negative world opinion. Instead, he took the offensive with wily propaganda assaults designed to blame Middle Eastern conflict on Israel.[82] Hussein consistently linked any withdrawal from Kuwait to an Israeli withdrawal from the West Bank and Gaza. The underlying premise to this gambit was to present Israel, not Iraq, as the aggressor in the Middle East. With this well-worn ploy Hussein hoped to rally a panoply of Arab sympathy and support. He aspired to forge Arab and world anti-Semitism into a weapon to destroy Israel and ultimately secure his quest for power.

As the world watched in horror Hussein launched missile after missile against Israel. No one could doubt his anti-Semitic intent. Israel was being attacked not because they were a part of the allied coalition battling Iraqi aggression, but because they were Jews. The attacks ceased only with the decisive military defeat of Saddam Hussein.

---

82. "Iraq Chief Sees 50–50 Chance for Peace," *The New York Times*, 3 December 1990, p. A6.

The aftermath of war places the United States in the precarious political position of Middle Eastern peacemaker. To maintain the tenuously fragile coalition of Arab states, the United States must balance Arab and Israeli interests. Any advantage that the U.S. allows the Arab world to gain over Israel lends tacit approval to anti-Semitism.

The military materiel that we have poured into our current Arab allies may put Israel at future risk. Today's allies could be tomorrow's enemies. The United States must not depart from its long-standing pro-Semitic stance.

As long as the United States opposes anti-Semitism this nation will remain under the blessing clause of Genesis 12:3. Deviation from pro-Semitism opens the door to divine discipline and cursing. This book repeatedly documents the danger of a national and personal policy of anti-Semitism.

Since American soldiers have fought and died in the Middle East, the only noble and sacred cause justifying such sacrifice is opposing anti-Semitism, preserving Israel as the only democratic country in the region, and evangelizing in the Middle East. By upholding these honorable principles our military has truly preserved the great freedom and blessings which God has so abundantly bestowed on the United States as a client nation.

Subject Index

Scripture Index

OLD TESTAMENT

GENESIS

JOSHUA

JUDGES

1 SAMUEL

2 SAMUEL

1 KINGS

2 KINGS

1 CHRONICLES

2 CHRONICLES

EZRA

New Testament

NOTES

3002